Praise for *Team Baseballs:*

"From the gilded trophy balls from last year's World Series, ... a way to mark a team and a season so as to defy the passage of time. Whether you collect team-signed baseballs, or intend to buy one, or only admire them from afar, this is the book for you. Authors Mitnick and Spence are the experts and will steer you clear of forgeries, facsimile balls, deceptive clubhouse signers, and a severe case of buyer's remorse."

—John Thorn, author of *Total Baseball*

"Team baseballs have always been a fascinating element of collecting because of the potential for forensics—you can often nail the exact date the ball was signed. John and Jim have delivered an authoritative look at this subject in a very entertaining way. Now where is my Black Sox ball with an 'X' for Joe Jackson??!!"

—Marty Appel, author of *Munson: The Life and Death of a Yankee Captain*

"Like broadcasters and ballparks, autographed baseballs forge connecting tissue between the public and The Game. The balls depicted in the many color illustrations evoke some of the greatest events and personalities in baseball history. A terrific book—and trip down memory lane."

—Curt Smith, author of *Voices of The Game* and *Storied Stadiums*

"John Mitnick and James Spence have provided a detailed instructive guide for collecting team-signed baseballs. Collecting these gems can be tricky—this book will show you how to avoid the many pitfalls."

—Peter Golenbock, author of *Dynasty: The New York Yankees, 1949–1964*

TEAM BASEBALLS

TEAM BASEBALLS

ARTIFACTS OF THE GAME

John M. Mitnick AND James J. Spence, Jr.

To Bobby Chen,
Enjoy our Hobby!

ARTIFACT PUBLISHING
McLean, Virginia

Artifact Publishing
P.O. Box 135
McLean, Virginia 22101

Disclaimer/Limitation of Liability: Authentication, valuation, and preservation of autographed material, including baseballs, involve the exercise of subjective judgment in each individual case based on knowledge that is constantly evolving. Nothing in this book shall be construed as advice regarding the authenticity, value, or preservation of any item or as investment or legal advice, and neither the authors nor the publisher shall have any liability whatsoever based on or relating to any information, statement, opinion, or illustration in this book.

ISBN: 978-0-615-36628-9
Library of Congress Control Number: 2010906594

Front cover: Detail of a 1924 World Series panoramic photograph showing the Washington Senators and New York Giants with President Calvin Coolidge and other dignitaries at the seventh and deciding game (Griffith Stadium, Washington, D.C., October 10, 1924), along with World Champion 1924 Senators (left) and National League Champion 1924 Giants (right) team baseballs.

Back cover: Panoramic photograph of the World Champion 1927 New York Yankees with images of a 1927 Yankees team baseball. (Team baseball photographs courtesy of Dr. Richard C. Angrist)

Edited, designed, typeset, and produced by Princeton Editorial Associates Inc., Scottsdale, Arizona. Photography for Gallery and various other illustrations by Alex Jamison Photography.

Printed in the United States of America on acid-free paper ∞

9 8 7 6 5 4 3 2 1

CONTENTS

PREFACE

This book began as a labor of love for collector John M. Mitnick during time off between his 1996 campaign for U.S. Congress and the resumption of his full-time law practice in January 1997. Over the following years he worked on the manuscript when time permitted, revising it as his research and developments in the market warranted. In 2007, having reached the decision to publish, he approached autograph authenticator and longtime friend James J. Spence, Jr., regarding possible co-authorship, and this work is the result of their ensuing collaboration. It is hoped that this book will introduce team baseballs to a wider audience of baseball fans and historians and assist collectors at all levels in developing their collections and preserving these artifacts of baseball history.

ACKNOWLEDGMENTS

My appreciation goes to my parents, Dr. Barbara and Howard Mitnick, and to my sister Jane for their love and support for my various scholastic, vocational, and avocational endeavors over the years, including this book. Special gratitude goes to my mother for sharing her formidable editorial skills and insights from her many years of distinguished scholarly publishing. I thank my grandparents for their love and inspiration, and particularly my grandfather, Sydney Jacobs, for helping to introduce me to baseball as a child. His sense of humor was renowned; as a nonagenarian he once teased me by saying that he had a 1927 Yankees team ball for me. Since he had actually seen Babe Ruth play, I almost fell for it. Last but not least, my fiancée, Dr. CarolDeane "Dee" Benedict, has cheerfully tolerated my many days of work on this project, even as she has coped with the demands of residency. She has my love and admiration always.

—John M. Mitnick

Heartfelt gratitude must be expressed to some special people in my life—to my wife, Michelle, who has endured countless hours of work that have robbed us of precious time together; to my grandfathers, Marty Mongelli, Charlie Di Natale, and James D. Spence, and my father James J. Spence, Sr., who inspired my life's vocation with their love for the game, collecting, and nostalgia; to my five siblings, Karen, Patti, Martin, Kathe, and Robb, who test my knowledge using Google; to my three sons James III ("Jimbo"),

Ryan ("Pooch"), and Harrison ("Willie"), the next generation of collectors and my ultimate motivations for success; and to my dear mother Kathleen, without whose love and encouragement I just might be working some job without a passion.

—James J. Spence, Jr.

INTRODUCTION

The one constant through all the years . . . has been baseball. America has rolled by like an army of steamrollers. It's been erased like a blackboard, rebuilt, and erased again. But baseball has marked the time. This field, this game, it's a part of our past. . . . It reminds us of all that once was good, and that could be again.

"Terence Mann" (played by James Earl Jones), *Field of Dreams,* Universal Studios, 1989

Field of Dreams is a baseball movie, laced with science fiction, which explores many themes that transcend the game—regret, atonement, redemption, unfulfilled dreams, the complex relationship between fathers and sons, standing up for one's beliefs in the face of adversity—the list goes on. Its overarching theme, however, is the innate human desire to celebrate and even relive the past.

Would any one of us pass up the opportunity to capture a moment in time, put it up on a shelf, and take it down whenever we want to relive it? As the world around us constantly changes and becomes more fast-paced, complex, and sometimes even dangerous, occasionally we find ourselves longing for the past and its seemingly simpler, happier times. Recalling historical events and heroes gives us comfort and helps to maintain our family relationships, friendships, and sense of community, even in the face of adversity. It keeps us firmly rooted in our identity and values as we confront the uncertainties of the present and the future.

In recent years, there has been a surge of interest in the history of baseball, one of our uniquely American institutions. For proof, look no further than the recent explosion in the number of books and films on baseball history. Some of the credit belongs to Ken Burns' epic *Baseball* video series, which debuted on public television stations in 1994 and has been rebroadcast periodically since then. Employing the innovative style of his previous *Civil War* series, including in-character narration and clever camera work using still images to simulate motion, Burns presented a course in baseball history in nine lectures. He emphasized the personalities and events that flesh out the raw statistics, placed baseball history within the overall context of American history, and effectively portrayed baseball as a continuing reflection of American culture. As Burns and his production partner Lynn Novick have put it so eloquently, "Nothing in our daily life offers more of the comfort of continuity, the generational connection of belonging to a vast and complicated American family, the powerful sense of home, the freedom from time's constraints, and the great gift of accumulated memory than does our National Pastime."[1]

Despite baseball's frequent controversies, the 2001 World Series proved that our national game still has the power to lift the spirits of the nation, even in times of crisis. The iconic symbolism of President George W. Bush walking to the pitcher's mound in Yankee Stadium to throw out the ceremonial first pitch—just seven weeks to the day after terrorists attacked New York City and Washington, D.C.—brought the crowd and the nation to its feet. It remains for the stakeholders in baseball—not just the team owners and players, but all Americans—as the present trustees of a national institution, to have the good sense to ensure that professional baseball continues and prospers.

Although the *Baseball* documentary was monumental in its scope, baseball nostalgia existed long before 1994. In fact, it has been around for as long as there has been something to be nostalgic about. One important manifestation has been the popularity of "Old Timers" gatherings at Major League ballparks since at least the early 1920s; another is the meteoric rise of interest in baseball memorabilia over the last 30 years.

Beginning in the late nineteenth century, various commercial concerns (most notably tobacco companies) began producing cards that depicted professional baseball players and other athletes and famous figures in an effort to promote their products, and baseball fans of all ages began collecting cards that featured their heroes. Later, certainly by the 1920s, a small but growing group of baseball enthusiasts began to collect players' autographs and other memorabilia. Their collecting interest was a hobby and an outgrowth of their personal connection with the game of baseball.

In the 1960s, however, something changed. A corps of serious adult baseball card collectors began to organize and form networks of contacts. Many of them became at least part-time dealers. In the 1970s, the phenomenon of the hobby convention or "card show" began to develop, and with it the rudiments of an organized market in vintage baseball cards. In 1973, the first periodical devoted to sports memorabilia collecting began regular publication. The first national convention was held in 1980, and the card shows soon grew into full-scale memorabilia shows, which included dealers and collectors buying and selling all kinds of baseball memorabilia (including equipment, uniforms, photographs, programs, tickets, and autographs) and present and former players participating in autograph sessions. Today's shows feature the memorabilia of all major professional sports (although baseball clearly dominates the market), and the largest shows attract hundreds of dealers and many thousands of collectors.

Among the many categories of baseball memorabilia is the team-signed baseball or "team ball." Beginning around 1910, Major League teams began to sign baseballs as mementos, at first in an ad hoc manner and in very small numbers, and later more regularly and in greater quantities. By the 1930s, all teams were signing baseballs on a regular basis during the season. The pens have changed over time, but the method has stayed the same: one by one the players, the manager, and the coaches physically pick up the ball and apply their unique signatures. The team ball thus has one characteristic that sets it apart from nearly all other vintage baseball memorabilia: the team members themselves create it.

The medium of presentation—an actual baseball that eventually becomes an antiquity in its own right—draws an immediate emotional response unlike any other autograph medium. The baseball itself is the ultimate symbol of the game. It represents better than anything else the enterprise in which the signatories were engaged, and in which they and their fans experienced triumph and tragedy, victory and defeat, elation and sorrow, and, of course, many sunny afternoons and electric evenings at the ballpark. By signing the ball, each signatory symbolically affirms that he is a member of the team at that moment in time and establishes a personal connection with the ball that will endure as long as it exists. As the signing of team balls has become more routine over time, certainly players have devoted less thought to the process—to the point where it has become just

Figure I.1. David Eckstein, 2006 World Series Most Valuable Player, presenting a 2006 St. Louis Cardinals World Championship team ball to President George W. Bush during a team visit to the White House, January 16, 2007. (Courtesy of the George W. Bush Presidential Library)

one of their normal activities—but that does not diminish the significance of the final product.

A team ball really is a miraculous thing. It literally affords a direct connection with specific teams, players, and events of the past. It can virtually transport the beholder back to the 1927 New York Yankees' "Murderers Row" with Babe Ruth and Lou Gehrig—or Connie Mack's great Philadelphia Athletics teams of the late 1920s and early 1930s—or the 1941 season, when a nation on the brink of war witnessed Ted Williams' .406 season and Joe DiMaggio's 56-game hitting streak—or Bill Mazeroski's Game Seven home run that won the 1960 World Series for the underdog Pittsburgh Pirates—or the 1969 "Miracle Mets." For skeptics, the authors recommend watching a World Series game (past or present) or a baseball documentary such as *When It Was a Game*, or listening to the audio version of *The Glory of Their Times*, with a few relevant team balls out on the coffee table. If the presence of the team balls does not enhance the experience, the pulse of the viewer should be taken forthwith to determine whether medical treatment is needed.

A team ball is truly an artifact of baseball history. As such, it is also an artifact of American history. Quite literally, it delivers history to your fingertips.

The number of collectors of team balls has surged in recent years. That surge has certainly coincided with the exploding interest in baseball history, but it has undoubtedly also been influenced by the general growth in autograph collecting. America's fascination with nostalgia probably has also fueled interest. Whatever the reasons, collecting team balls is now very popular among baseball memorabilia enthusiasts, and its popularity is growing constantly.

This book provides a comprehensive guide to collecting team balls to coincide with their first centennial. The topics addressed are very important, but many have received little or no attention in hobby publications. The authors' objective was to produce a guide that will be useful for beginners and advanced collectors alike. It is intended to help collectors choose their purchases wisely and then organize and preserve their collections. Although the focus is on team balls, it is important to note that much of the content of this book is applicable to all varieties of signed baseballs, including the very popular single-signature balls.

One of the attractive features of collecting team balls is that they come in all price ranges. If one does not have a lot of money to spend, one can start with the less expensive balls. At the time of publication, some team balls in decent condition from as far back as the 1950s can still be purchased for less than $100. As one acquires the knowledge (and the resulting confidence) as well as the resources to purchase more valuable balls, they can be pursued into the tens of thousands of dollars—and perhaps beyond.

Another attractive feature of collecting team balls is that new ones are constantly being created. Every spring, each Major League team reinvents itself for another try at a pennant. The rosters change, and new team balls are signed during the season. As long as there is baseball, there will be new team balls created every year that will recall records, triumphs, and excitement of which we cannot yet conceive.

While the primary benefit of collecting team balls is the enjoyment of baseball history, there is a side benefit that is not insubstantial. Team balls (particularly the rare and top-condition pieces that are in highest demand) have risen dramatically in price in recent years, and that trend does not show any sign of abating despite the fluctuations of the economy. If recent price trends continue and a collector is careful in choosing purchases and preserving his or her collection, it will probably significantly appreciate in value over time. Collecting team balls thus affords the best of both worlds—it provides enjoyment and can be a good investment as well. One thing is certain: team balls, like other "tangibles" (to use a popular investment term), and unlike many investments, are not subject to accounting scandals or counterparty risk.

One note of caution must be mentioned. As in the case of other collectibles, collecting team balls is not for the uninformed. Aside from "clubhouse" signatures (non-authentic signatures signed by a team employee), which appear all too frequently on team balls, and the (often unintentional) attempted passing-off of stamped-signature ("facsimile") balls as the real thing, with the advance of prices has come the inevitable appearance of forgeries. Non-authentic signatures on actual signed team balls are still the exception, but they are very expensive traps for the unwary. One should not do any less research, or obtain any less expert assistance, in purchasing a team ball than in purchasing a similarly valued painting or piece of antique furniture or jewelry. As in any field of antiques or collectibles, it is only prudent to become educated before investing money in team balls, and the primary purpose of this book is to assist the reader in acquiring or enhancing that education.

Apart from addressing the particulars of collecting, another purpose of this book is to recognize and celebrate team balls as artifacts of baseball history. With baseball fans and historians in mind, the authors have included many illustrations of historically significant team balls. It is hoped that those images will evoke memories of great teams, moments, and personalities in the history of our national game.

Thank you for purchasing this book. The authors welcome correspondence. You can contact John M. Mitnick by e-mail at jmitnick@teambaseballs.com, and James J. Spence, Jr., at jspence@spenceloa.com. Additional copies of this book may be purchased at www.spenceloa.com.

Note

1. http://www.pbs.org/kenburns/baseball/about/.

ONE

WHAT IS A TEAM BASEBALL?

Have you ever seen the baseballs stamped with players' signatures at the concession stands at Major League ballparks? Did you ever think that they were genuine signatures? Have you ever wondered if authentic team-signed baseballs exist?

As a child in the early 1970s, John Mitnick had the pleasure of attending many New York Mets games at Shea Stadium with his grandfather and parents, and like many kids then and now he would try to get players' autographs before the game, usually on a program, but occasionally on a baseball. In those days, players seemed more willing to sign autographs at the stadium than they are today (with some notable exceptions, such as Cal Ripken, Jr.). He could never have dreamed then of obtaining the signatures of the entire team on a ball. The closest that he ever came was a facsimile ball of the 1969 Mets, which his grandfather and parents purchased for him at the first Major League baseball game he ever attended in 1969. He still has that ball.

Only as an adult did he learn that authentic team-signed baseballs (or "team balls") actually exist. In fact, teams have been signing them for a century now, there is a very active market for them today, and they are available for purchase from numerous sources. If you are intrigued by the history, drama, and memories that can be evoked by collecting team balls, then read on.

DEFINITION

By definition, a team ball is simply a baseball signed by the members of a baseball team. Although there is no consensus on the minimum number of signatures necessary for a signed baseball to be considered a team ball, clearly more than just a few are required. Some collectors insist on a minimum of 20 signatures from a professional team, but while 20 is a reasonable quantitative benchmark to use as a rule of thumb, a collector should not be inflexible. The definition of a team ball should be qualitative rather than quantitative: a signed baseball should be considered a team ball not because it has a certain number of signatures, but rather because the signatures on the ball collectively represent an entire team rather than a mere assemblage of individuals. Normally that will require 20 or more signatures, but a collector should be flexible regarding the number of signatures and should be primarily concerned with substance over quantity.

What does it take to achieve that substance? In the authors' view, an ideal team ball should, at a minimum, have the signatures of the entire starting lineup, all starting pitchers, the team's "closer," and any "key signatures" not already included in those categories. A key signature is a team member's autograph that is essential for the completeness of a team ball because of one or more of the following factors:

1. His general status in the game of baseball (e.g., a member or likely future member of the Hall of Fame);
2. His significance to a particular team because of a specific event (e.g., Bobby Thomson on a 1951 Giants team ball because of his famous walk-off home run in the deciding game of the playoff series against the Dodgers that won the 1951 National League pennant for the Giants, or Don Larsen on a 1956 Yankees team ball because of his perfect game pitched in Game Five of the 1956 World Series);
3. His significance in a particular season (e.g., a Most Valuable Player, Cy Young, or Rookie of the Year award winner);
4. His notoriety for some other reason in or outside baseball; or
5. The rarity of his signature.

If a ball has most, but not all, of those signatures, it is still certainly worthy of consideration as a team ball. It must be recognized that nearly all team balls are missing the signatures of at least a few roster players, for many possible reasons. Those reasons include a player's refusal or failure to sign before the balls are distributed, the periodic absence of a player due to injury or illness, player trades, and the assignment of players to and from the minor leagues over the course of a season. The definition of a team ball takes into account the reality that team balls are almost never totally complete, and balls that are missing one or more of the signatures required for an ideal team ball are routinely marketed and accepted by collectors as team balls. A collector should visualize the universe of team balls as a spectrum: the most complete ideal examples of team balls are at one end of the spectrum; the examples that are minimally complete for consideration as team balls are at the other end; and examples with intermediate levels of completeness are in between.

The overwhelming majority of signed balls that are marketed as team balls have between 20 and 30 signatures. There is one thing on which all team ball collectors agree when it comes to signatures—the more, the better. Some teams in history are notorious among collectors for having produced team balls with only 15–18 signatures (the St. Louis Cardinals of the mid-1930s and the Los Angeles Dodgers of the late 1970s readily come to mind) that often included the starters and any other key signatures, and those balls should be considered true team balls in accordance with our qualitative definition. Indeed, from certain teams, a ball with that number of signatures might be the best one can find. Each collector must decide whether a particular ball truly represents a particular team and is worth adding to his or her collection.

The rest of this chapter defines and introduces the various types of team balls. Discussions of the related topics of other multisignature baseballs, single-signature baseballs, other team-signed baseball-related items, and team-signed balls from other sports are also included.

MAJOR LEAGUE TEAM BALLS

Regular Season Team Balls

By far the largest category of team balls are those signed by Major League teams, and we refer to them as "regular season" team balls. There are two subcategories of regular season team balls: original season team balls and reunion team balls.

Original Season Team Balls

We refer to team balls signed during the original year in which a team was playing as "original season" team balls, and they make up the overwhelming majority of regular season team balls. Major League teams have the resources to purchase large quantities of baseballs for signing, and the demand is high for balls from Major League teams in order to supply players and coaches, dignitaries, team employees, and charity auctions. As a result of frequent expansion, there are now 30 Major League teams, and each one signs team balls just about every day of the regular season (whether home or away) and often during spring training as well. The teams that participate in postseason play sign even more balls, especially if they make it to the World Series.

The present high rate of team ball production did not always exist (see Chapter Two), but balls signed by today's teams are relatively plentiful (although not necessarily inexpensive) in comparison with the early years, and many of them reach the market through various channels. That said, there is recent anecdotal evidence that the number of new team balls being produced by some teams is declining for several reasons, including some star players' refusal to sign in the clubhouse.

Reunion Team Balls

Occasionally reunions of teams are held at which the attendees sign team balls. Such occasions are usually organized by a Major League franchise or an enterprising autograph show promoter to celebrate a special event (such as the anniversary of a championship team), and the balls signed at reunions are appropriately referred to as "reunion" team balls.

In nearly all cases, reunions are held only for championship teams. One notable exception was a reunion of the inaugural 1962 New York Mets, who finished with the inauspicious record of 40-120. Apparently, in order to rate a reunion, a team has to be either very good or very bad and colorful (and, in the latter case, perhaps from New York). An early example of a reunion of a championship team was an apparent reunion of the World Champion 1940 Cincinnati Reds, which was held sometime around 1960 and at which some very complete team balls were signed. Figure 1.1 shows a team ball signed at that reunion and an original season 1940 Reds team ball for comparison. The World Champion 1948 Cleveland Indians apparently held a reunion sometime in the 1960s, because a few (albeit incomplete)

Figure 1.1. 1940 Cincinnati Reds reunion circa 1960 (left) and original season (right) team balls (World Champions).

reunion balls from that team, which were apparently signed during that time period, have emerged in the market. Figure 1.2 shows a 1948 Indians reunion team ball alongside an original season 1948 Indians team ball.

In the case of very early championship teams, reunion balls might be the only means of obtaining a team ball. Figure 1.3 depicts an extremely rare reunion ball signed in 1925 by the 1901 National League Champion

Figure 1.2. 1948 Cleveland Indians reunion circa 1960s (left) and original season (right) team balls (World Champions).

Pittsburgh Pirates. It is safe to say that it would be impossible to find a ball signed by that team in 1901. Figure 1.4 shows a rare reunion ball signed around 1951 by members of the National League Champion 1916 Brooklyn Robins. A few original team balls from that team might exist, but they would be extremely rare.

In recent years, autograph show promoters have organized reunion shows at which team balls were signed featuring the 1960 Pittsburgh Pirates, the 1961 New York Yankees, the 1968 Detroit Tigers, the 1969 New York Mets, the 1978 New York Yankees, the 1979 Pittsburgh Pirates, the 1980 Philadelphia Phillies, and the 1986 New York Mets. For some of those teams, there have been multiple reunions. Note that all of them were World Championship teams; reunions are privately promoted only when a promoter's economic analysis suggests that a profit can be made (i.e., only in cases in which there will be a sufficient level of interest on the part of the public in attending the reunion and purchasing memorabilia produced at

Figure 1.3. 1901 Pittsburgh Pirates reunion team ball (National League Champions) signed in 1925, possibly the earliest team ball (in terms of the team represented) in existence.

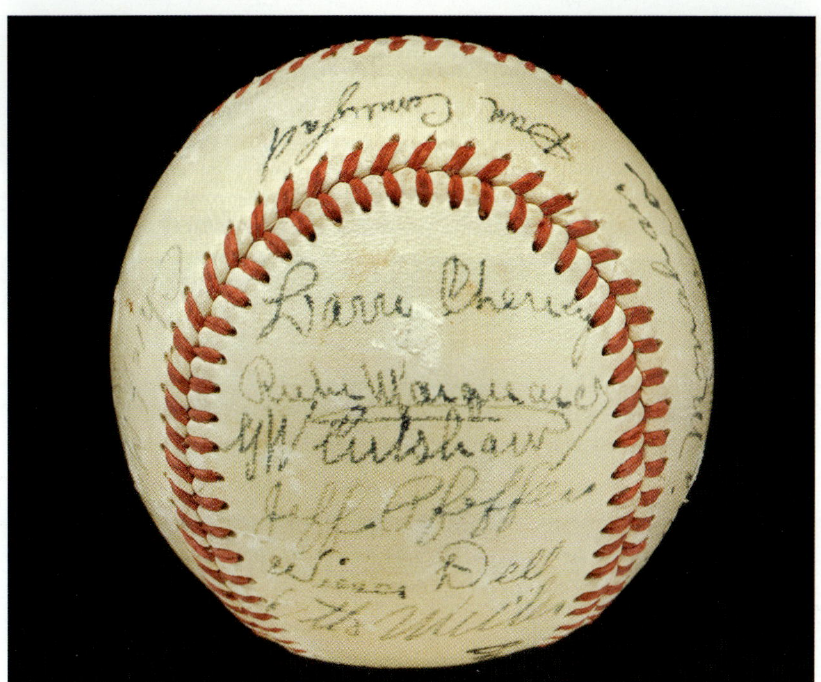

Figure 1.4. 1916 Brooklyn Robins reunion team ball (National League Champions), circa 1951.

the event, such as team balls, in order to make the reunion profitable). That level of interest usually exists only in the case of championship teams, because such reunions celebrate a significant historical event.

Although reunion team balls certainly can have significant value and can be legitimate examples of team balls from the teams that they represent, they lack the originality—and therefore, all else being equal, the full value—of original season team balls. Therefore, collectors should know how to differentiate between them (see Chapter Three).

All-Star Team Balls

All-Star team balls are a separate category of Major League team balls. Early precursors of today's All-Star Games featured ad hoc teams made up of "star" players, such as the Addie Joss benefit game held on July 24, 1911, and the Tim Murnane benefit game held at Boston's Fenway Park on September 27, 1917. What we know today as the annual Major League

Baseball All-Star Game began in 1933; each summer since 1933 (except 1945), the Major Leagues have held an All-Star Game that pitted the best (or in some cases the most popular) players of the National League against those of the American League. Two separate All-Star Games were held in four years (1959–1962). The signing of team balls was a well-established practice by 1933, so it is not surprising that All-Star teams have always signed team balls when they gathered in the host city for the game. Figures 1.5, 1.6, and 1.7 show American League All-Star team balls from 1933, 1934, and 1935, respectively.

All-Star team balls are obviously much rarer than regular season team balls, because they can be signed only on one or two days of the season during the All-Star break, and therefore the number of team balls produced is naturally very limited. They are also particularly desirable because of the caliber of players who are selected to be All-Stars, and because, as they age, they tend to include the signatures of numerous members of the Hall of

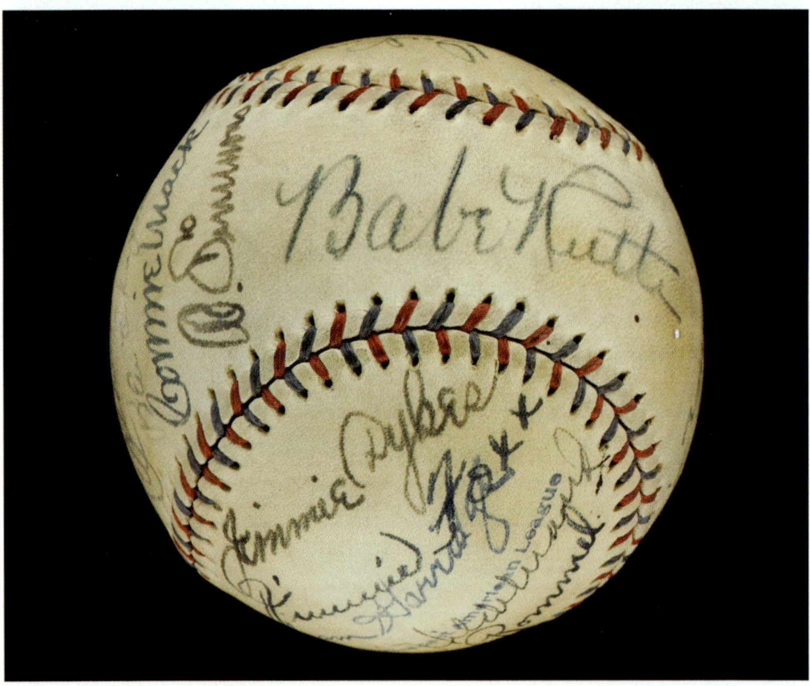

Figure 1.5. 1933 American League All-Star team ball, signed by the winners of the inaugural All-Star Game held at Chicago's Comiskey Park on July 6, 1933.

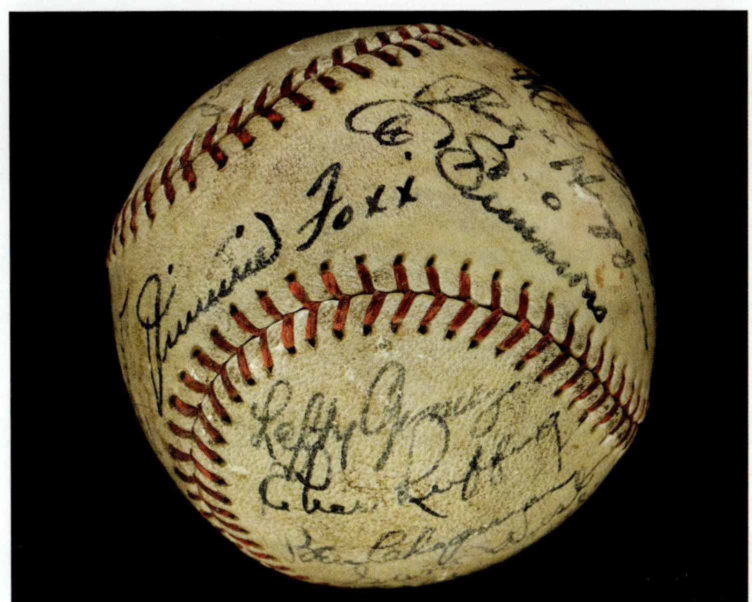

Figure 1.6. 1934 American League All-Star team ball, signed by the victors, although National League pitcher Carl Hubbell amazingly struck out sluggers Ruth, Gehrig, Foxx, Simmons, and Cronin consecutively.

Figure 1.7. 1935 American League All-Star team ball, signed by the team that made it three All-Star Game victories in a row for the American League.

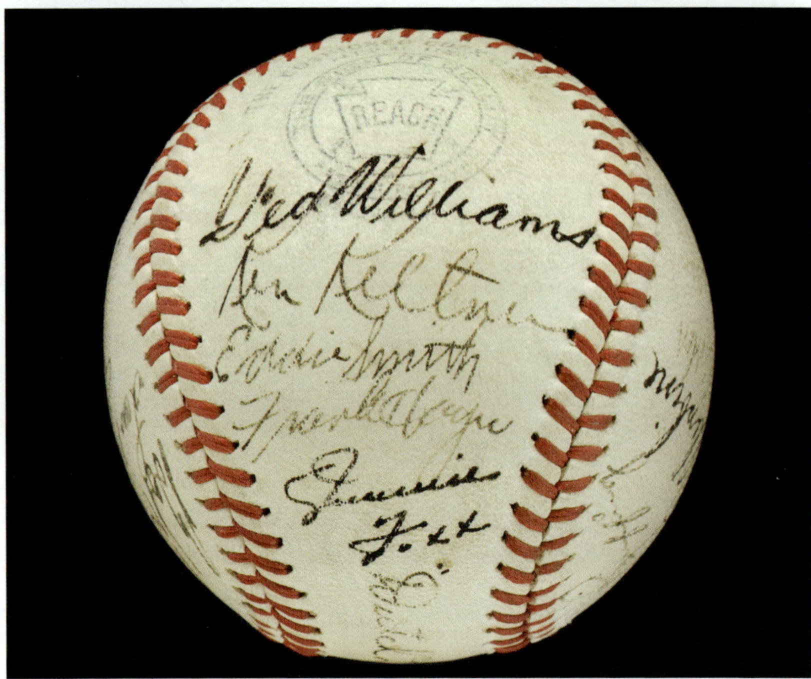

Figure 1.8. 1941 American League All-Star team ball, including the signature of a 22-year-old Ted Williams, who won the game with a walk-off home run in the bottom of the ninth inning.

Fame. They might also be particularly attractive to collectors if a significant event occurred in the game (for example, Ted Williams' game-winning home run in the ninth inning of the 1941 All-Star Game; see Figure 1.8). It is the opinion of the authors that All-Star team balls are generally undervalued in today's marketplace, largely because of most collectors' focus on regular season team balls, and therefore they represent a good opportunity for investment appreciation over time as more collectors come to recognize their value.

NEGRO LEAGUE TEAM BALLS

Throughout the late nineteenth century and the first half of the twentieth century, many all-black professional and semiprofessional baseball teams played throughout the United States. Some of them organized into leagues;

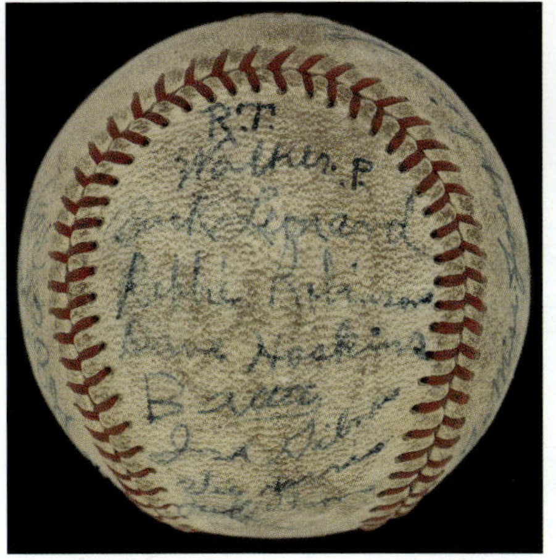

Figure 1.9. 1945 Homestead Grays Negro League team ball, featuring Hall of Fame members James "Cool Papa" Bell, Josh Gibson, and Buck Leonard. (Courtesy of Legendary Auctions)

the first one to succeed was the Negro National League organized by Andrew "Rube" Foster in 1920. Until the racial integration of the game, which finally began with the signing of Jackie Robinson by the Brooklyn Dodgers organization in 1945, some of the nation's finest baseball talent resided in the Negro Leagues. Some team balls exist from Negro League teams, but they are extraordinarily rare. Figure 1.9 depicts a team ball from the 1945 Homestead Grays, who won their ninth consecutive Negro National League title that season; it features the signatures of Hall of Fame members James "Cool Papa" Bell, Josh Gibson, and Buck Leonard.

MINOR LEAGUE AND OTHER TEAM BALLS

Minor league teams have been signing team balls for almost as long as Major League teams, but in much smaller quantities. Team balls are also signed at minor league all-star games, just as in the Major Leagues.

Although minor league team balls are certainly interesting items of baseball memorabilia, they generally do not generate significant interest or attain substantial monetary value unless they contain signatures of players who went on to noteworthy careers in the Major Leagues. In that case they can be very valuable as rare, early examples of future stars' signatures.

For example, Figure 1.10 shows a very rare minor league team ball from the 1930s that features the signature of a young Pee Wee Reese, a future member of the Hall of Fame. Figure 1.11 depicts a 1941 Rochester Red Wings team ball signed by future immortal Stan Musial at his last minor league stop on the way to the St. Louis Cardinals toward the end of that season. Figure 1.12 shows a 1951 Kansas City Blues team ball with Mickey Mantle, signed during his last brief stint in the minor leagues. Minor league team balls can also attain significant monetary value if they contain the signatures of minor league managers and coaches who previously had noteworthy careers in the Major Leagues.

The preceding general statements also apply to team balls signed by amateur teams, such as college teams, and Olympic teams. They can be very interesting and desirable collectibles, especially when they contain signatures of members of the Hall of Fame and otherwise famous players.

Now, with a firm grounding in the types of team balls that are available, we are ready to move on to Chapters Two through Nine and explore the history of team balls and how to acquire, classify, authenticate, value, manage, and protect one's collection. We conclude this chapter with brief notes on certain topics related to team balls.

Figure 1.10. Minor league team ball with Pee Wee Reese, possibly a collection of 1939 American Association all-stars.

Figure 1.11. 1941 Rochester Red Wings minor league team ball with Stan Musial.

Figure 1.12. 1951 Kansas City Blues minor league team ball with Mickey Mantle.

A NOTE ON OTHER MULTISIGNATURE BASEBALLS

Although team balls constitute the majority of the multisignature balls that exist, there are several other types.

Hall of Fame Induction Balls

The first Baseball Hall of Fame induction ceremonies were held in Cooperstown, New York, in 1939. Beginning in that year, and at each succeeding year's ceremonies, the new inductees, joined by previously inducted Hall of Fame members and often some invited former players who were not members, would sign baseballs. At first, signed balls were obtained in small numbers by attendees who brought balls and asked the inductees to sign them. Those balls, particularly the ones from the 1939 induction, command huge prices; an example from 1939 with all 11 original Hall of Fame inductees sold for $63,000 at Christie's East in September 1997.

Later on, certainly by the 1960s, the signing at the ceremonies became more organized, with balls signed in quantity and then distributed to the members and other dignitaries to take home as souvenirs of the occasion. Hall of Fame induction balls from the last three decades have remained relatively inexpensive. The signatures on them are often not particularly rare, and, without a connection like a championship to draw collectors to them, they have not risen in value nearly as much as many team balls. Collecting recent Hall of Fame induction balls is, however, an excellent way to obtain the authentic signatures of many of baseball's greatest players of all time at a low cost per signature. It is the authors' opinion that, in the years to come, such balls should appreciate in value significantly, and such appreciation is already beginning to occur.

Special Event and Old Timers Day Balls

Since at least the 1920s, there have been gatherings of "Old Timers" (retired Major League players) at Major League ballparks. Some of the first Old Timers gatherings were reunions of former championship teams. Those gatherings were sporadic at first, but by the 1950s many teams had added an "Old Timers Day" to their annual schedules, to which they invited

Figure 1.13. Ball signed at a tribute to Washington Senators owner Clark Griffith at Griffith Stadium on August 17, 1948.

former team members and other former players to participate in a pregame ceremony and even play an inning or two in an "Old Timers Game."

Baseballs have often been signed at Old Timers and other special events, and even though there is often no theme, those balls, particularly the ones from the 1920s through the 1950s, often contain some very rare and valuable signatures. Figure 1.13 shows a ball from a Washington Senators event held at Griffith Stadium on August 17, 1948, at which Clark Griffith, the longtime owner and president of the Senators, was honored; that ball includes the signatures of Griffith, baseball commissioner Albert B. "Happy" Chandler, and other Hall of Fame members Joe Cronin, Goose Goslin, and Sam Rice, among others.

Theme Balls

A "theme ball" is a multisignature ball that includes only the signatures of players who have a certain accomplishment in common or another significant connection. Examples include balls signed by players who have hit 500 or more home runs or accumulated 3,000 hits, pitchers with 300 or more wins or who have pitched no-hitters, those who have won Most Valuable Player or Rookie of the Year awards, and players who had a special connection as teammates (e.g., Babe Ruth and Lou Gehrig, Mickey Mantle and Roger Maris, Sandy Koufax and Don Drysdale). Figure 1.14 depicts a baseball signed by Babe Ruth and Lou Gehrig, and Figure 1.15 shows a baseball signed by Mickey Mantle and Roger Maris. Figure 1.16 shows a very rare ball signed in the late 1970s or early 1980s by the two men who broke Babe Ruth's single-season and career home run records: Roger Maris and Hank Aaron, respectively.

Many theme balls have been produced in recent years by creative autograph show promoters. They are interesting items to collect, but they are usually produced in large numbers and generally have not risen very much in value above their initial selling prices. It does not help that some theme balls (particularly the 500 home run hitter balls) have become favorite subjects for forgers. Figure 1.17 shows a side-by-side comparison of authentic and forged 500 home run theme balls. It is probable, however, that even theme balls produced in quantity will appreciate in value as time passes.

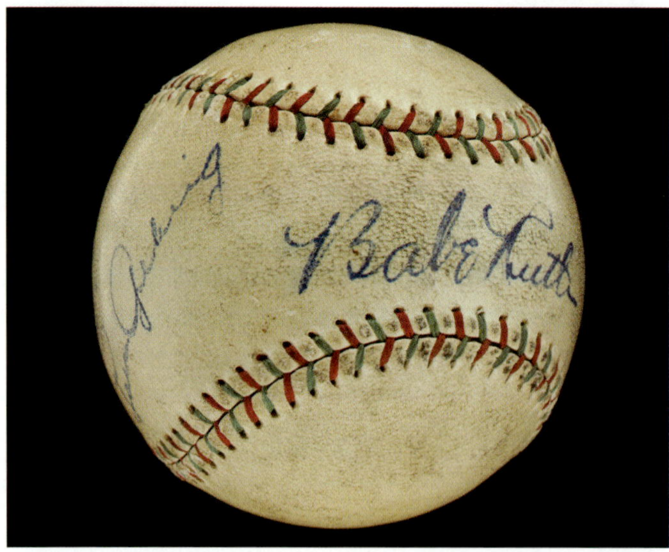

Figure 1.14. Theme ball signed by legendary New York Yankees sluggers Babe Ruth and Lou Gehrig (circa 1929).

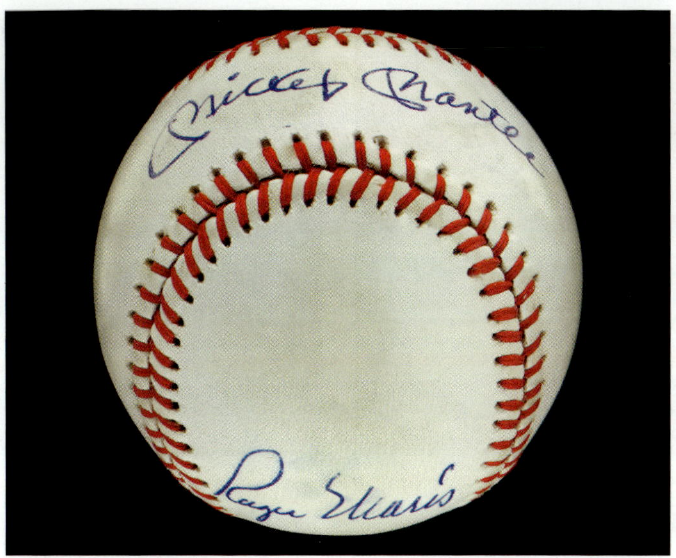

Figure 1.15. Theme ball signed by New York Yankees teammates Mickey Mantle and Roger Maris, who battled for the single-season home run record in 1961 (circa early 1980s).

Figure 1.16. Theme ball signed by Hank Aaron and Roger Maris as then-reigning career and single-season home run record holders, respectively (circa early 1980s).

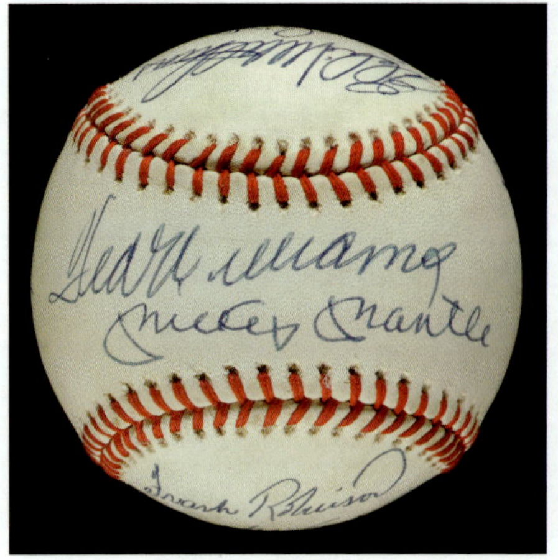

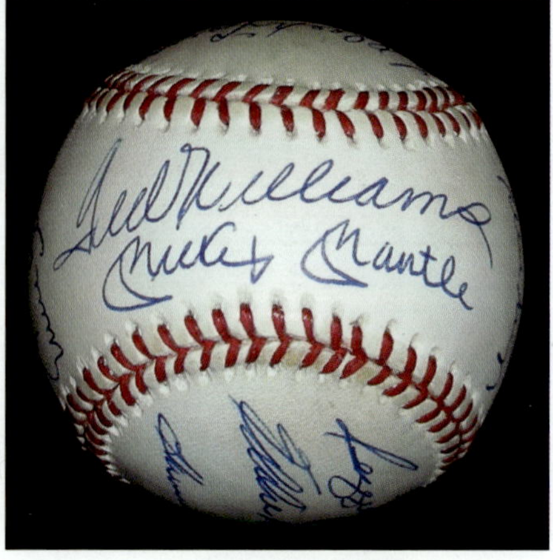

Figure 1.17. Authentic (left) and forged (right) 500 home run hitter theme balls. These balls have become favorite subjects for forgers.

A NOTE ON SINGLE-SIGNATURE BASEBALLS

A single-signature baseball is simply a baseball signed by only one person. A few single-signature balls date from the dawn of team balls in the 1910s (see Chapter Two), but they are extremely rare. For example, Figure 1.18 shows a ball signed and dated by Honus Wagner in 1916. Yet it was unquestionably Babe Ruth who first popularized the concept of the single-signature ball. "The Babe" was the first, and for a while virtually the only, player whose signature on a baseball was in high demand by fans, and he signed many thousands of balls during and after his playing career. Ruth developed the signing of the sweet spot of a baseball into a virtual art form with his bold and distinctive signature. Figure 1.19 depicts a classic Ruth signature on the sweet spot of a Babe Ruth "Home Run Special" baseball manufactured by Reach.

Judging from extant examples, Ruth began to sign baseballs for fans in significant numbers in the mid-1920s, when his fame soared (although there are a few examples that date from as early as 1918; see Figure 1.20). By the mid- to late 1920s, other present and former stars were being asked to sign baseballs, including Ty Cobb, Walter Johnson, and Honus Wagner, but

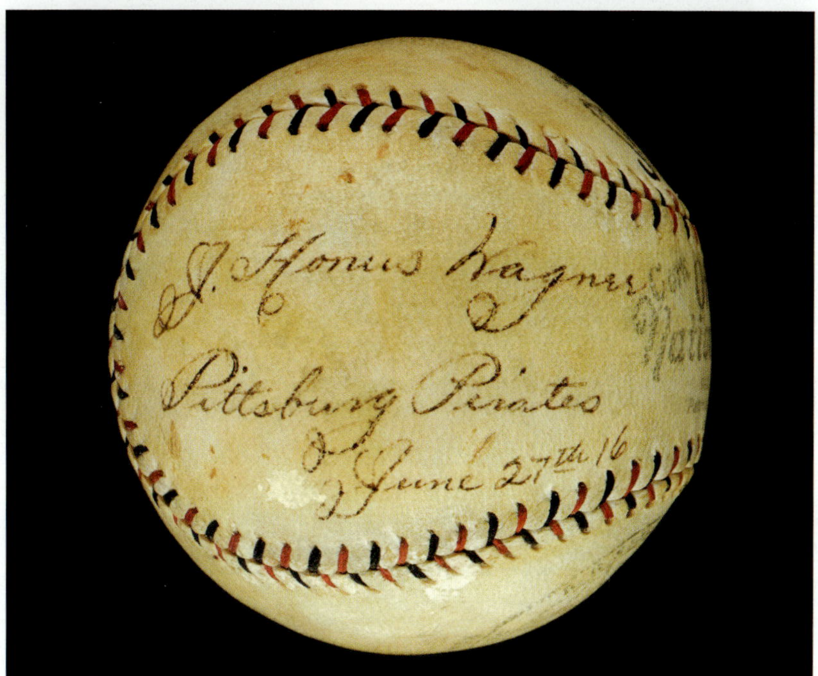

Figure 1.18. Honus Wagner single-signature ball, signed and dated by Wagner on June 27, 1916, and one of the earliest single-signature balls known. On that day the Chicago Cubs swept a double-header from Wagner's Pittsburgh Pirates at Weeghman Park (now Wrigley Field) in Chicago.

demand for Babe Ruth signatures unquestionably started the trend. By the 1930s, fans wielding baseballs and pens were seeking the autographs of many different star players, but single-signature balls continued to be created in much smaller numbers than team balls. The reason is simple: by the late 1920s, teams were signing team balls on a regular basis in the clubhouse, while single-signature balls were generally created only when a motivated fan with a baseball and a pen managed to meet a player in person or to obtain a signed ball by mail or through a friend (and then resist the temptation to add other players' signatures to the same ball)—which was not a common occurrence. That imbalance persisted until the advent of the sports memorabilia market in the early 1980s, with its autograph shows and private signing sessions, which began to produce mass quantities of single-

Figure 1.19. Babe Ruth single-signature ball signed during his playing career (circa 1932–1933).

Figure 1.20. Early Babe Ruth single-signature ball (circa 1918). (Courtesy of Legendary Auctions)

signature balls. For that reason, single-signature balls of virtually all players who died prior to the mid-1980s are uncommon.

Babe Ruth's stature is such that the Babe Ruth single-signature baseball has become symbolic of the game of baseball itself and the ultimate icon of baseball memorabilia. Perhaps in part for those reasons, the value of top-condition Babe Ruth "singles" has soared in recent years. The present record auction price was set at $87,720 in August 2005, although another Ruth ball—which is thought by some to be the finest example known—reportedly changed hands for $150,000 in a private transaction in September 2005. Like most other records, that one seems destined to be broken again and again in the future. Even lesser-condition Ruth singles have significant value, despite the relatively large number of balls that exist, because the demand is so high. Incidentally, the current record price paid for a single-signature baseball at public auction belongs not to a Babe Ruth ball, but rather to a ball signed by Hall of Fame pitcher Christy Mathewson, which sold for $161,000 in March 2007 (Figure 1.21).

Figure 1.21. Christy Mathewson single-signature ball, which sold for a record $161,000 in March 2007. (Courtesy of Huggins & Scott Auctions)

Not only was Babe Ruth the first to popularize the single-signature ball, he was also involved in the creation of the first theme balls. The first such balls produced in significant numbers were those signed by Ruth and fellow Yankees superstar Lou Gehrig in the late 1920s and early 1930s. Ruth and Gehrig made up the heart of the Yankees' overpowering "Murderers Row" lineup of that period, and, despite their personality differences, the two men were inextricably linked in the minds of fans. Ruth-Gehrig theme balls first came into being during postseason barnstorming tours led by the two stars and were signed for or sold to fans at tour stops around the country. They became prized souvenirs for each of the few fans who were fortunate enough to obtain one and, like Ruth "singles," have often been handed down from generation to generation. To this day, Ruth-Gehrig balls often turn up in remote locations around the country because local residents obtained them when the two stars and their teams came through town on one of their famous tours.

While signers of single-signature baseballs have traditionally been Major League players (or other baseball personalities, such as sportscasters and umpires), for many years collectors have procured signatures on baseballs from celebrities outside the realm of baseball. The first such non-baseball celebrities to sign balls were probably U.S. presidents. They became associated with the game once the tradition of the president throwing out the first ball on the opening day of the season was begun by President William Howard Taft on April 14, 1910. Figure 1.22 shows a baseball signed by Taft on May 2, 1910, at Pittsburgh's Forbes Field, and Figure 1.23 depicts a ball signed by Ronald Reagan during his presidency. Over the years, the variety of non-baseball celebrities who have been called on to sign baseballs has expanded, with balls being signed by stars from other sports, entertainers, astronauts, and U.S. and foreign political and military leaders. Figure 1.24 shows a ball signed and dated by General John "Blackjack" Pershing on April 13, 1921.

A more in-depth discussion of single-signature balls is beyond the scope of this book, although much of the information presented here is directly applicable to single-signature balls as well as team balls, including the key chapters on authentication and preservation, storage, and collection management. One point should be made clearly, however: *the markets for team balls and single-signature balls are separate and distinct.* The collector bases for the two categories certainly overlap (i.e., there are plenty of collectors

Figure 1.22. President William Howard Taft single-signature ball, signed at Pittsburgh's Forbes Field on May 2, 1910. (Courtesy of James W. Ancel, Sr., and the Louisville Slugger Museum & Factory)

Figure 1.23. President Ronald Reagan single-signature ball (1987). Presidential signed baseballs have become sought-after collectibles.

Figure 1.24. General John J. Pershing single-signature ball, signed on April 13, 1921, at an opening day game in Washington, D.C., between the Washington Senators and the Boston Red Sox. Pershing probably attended the game as the guest of President Warren G. Harding, who threw out the first ball.

who collect both types of balls), but each type of signed ball is in a separate market category of baseball memorabilia, with its own supply, demand, and pricing. Any attempt to draw comparisons between the two categories for valuation purposes would be useless.

Nothing illustrates the last point better than the fact that vintage team balls are almost always worth substantially less than the sum of the values of single-signature balls of the same players (or even just one or two of the key players)—which is counterintuitive to most of those who are not familiar with the valuation of signed baseballs. The reason is, quite simply, the separateness of the markets and the relative scarcity of single-signature balls of players who died before the mid-1980s.

A NOTE ON OTHER TEAM-SIGNED BASEBALL-RELATED ITEMS

Although baseballs are by far the most popular media for team signings, for many years Major League teams have signed other objects as mementos as well, including photographs, bats, and game programs. Examples are depicted in Figure 1.25.

Figure 1.25. 1942 St. Louis Cardinals team-signed photograph (top); 1940 Cincinnati Reds team-signed bat (bottom). Both teams were World Champions.

(figure continued on next page)

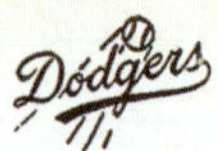

The 1962 National League campaign saw **DON DRYSDALE** go from the role of a controversial baseball figure to one of the game's great stars. Winner of the Cy Young Award as the top pitcher in baseball, Don led the majors in victories (25), innings pitched (314), starts (41) and strikeouts (232). The strong-armed San Fernando Valley native had come into his own and, at the age of 26, boasted more than one hundred victories. Most of Drysdale's individual statistics for 1963 are just as impressive. Only his victory total dropped and this can be traced to the amazing string of low-scoring games behind him. When Don dropped his fifteenth game in late August a review of his defeats showed only twenty-eight runs scored by the Dodgers. A team man all the way, Don took it philosophically. "I don't care as long as we win the pennant."

Rated one of the soundest batters in baseball, **TOMMY DAVIS** won the National League hitting title in his third season in the majors. There was not a hotter batter from April to September as the former Brooklyn baseball-basketball schoolboy star, made 230 hits, batted .346 and drove in 153 runs. Only three players in the history of the league—Hack Wilson, Chuck Klein and Joe Medwick—had ever topped that RBI-count. At his best when the competition is keenest, Davis has picked on the Dodgers' chief rival, the Giants, for some of his most devastating blasting. Once again in '63 Davis was the club's leading hitter and producer of runs, going into the stretch and very much in the running for the batting crown.

MAURY WILLS brought the stolen base back into baseball and became one of baseball's most discussed players during an amazing campaign of larceny in 1962. Operating throughout the '63 campaign on a taped left ankle (result of a first-game collision at the plate), Maury was unable to match his thievery of the non-pennant season but don't bet he won't be set to fly this October. Winner of awards that ranged from "Sporting News" Player-of-the-Year honors to a citation by the inmates of Folsom Prison as "Thief-of-the-Year," Maury wiped marks out of the record book which had almost been forgotten. Stealing 104 bases, he topped the 96 stolen by Ty Cobb as well as Bob Bescher's 51-year-old N.L. record of 80. To avoid an asterisk, Maury purloined 97 in 156 games, Cobb's record having been set in that many Detroit games. Along the way, Maury made 208 hits.

Heir-apparent to the Cy Young Award, **SANDY KOUFAX** has gained the plateau denied him a year ago by an injured finger. Seemingly headed for an all-time strikeout record and a 20-plus season in '62, Sandy was sidelined July 17 with a 14-and-5 record. He made a late-season comeback but to no avail. His woes were soon forgotten in '63 as he produced one pitching gem after another, became the first 20-game winner in the majors, fired the second no-hit, no-run game of his career (over the Giants, yet!), had ten shutouts going into September and an earned run average under two runs per game. This was the Sandy who would have put the Dodgers in the World Series of 1962. Koufax set a new National League strikeout record this year, breaking his own 269 mark (set in 1961) and became the first flinger in the league since Christy Mathewson (1903-04-05) to fan 200-or-more three successive seasons.

Baseball's two greatest exponents of the tape-measure home run vie in this World Series of 1963—the Yankee's Mickey Mantle and the Dodgers **FRANK HOWARD.** You can start a lively argument when you declare that a Mantle home run in Washington was longer than a Howard blast in Pittsburgh—now they meet head-on! Top home run hitter for the Dodgers the last two campaigns, "Hondo" stirs up a crowd just walking to the plate and leaves them stirred whether he goes down swinging or connects for the long ball. Benched now and then when his strikeouts become too numerous, Howard can be the roughest rapper on the club when he's in one of his hot streaks. In late August this year he hit five homers in eight games, including one as a pinch hitter. In a game against Milwaukee in July he swung at the first pitch twice, sending both sailing over the fences.

Shortly after the World Series, **JIM GILLIAM** will celebrate his thirty-fifth birthday. Somewhere along the line the guy who used to be called "Junior" must have sipped from the Fountain of Youth. A remarkably consistent performer ever since he became a full-fledged Dodger in 1953, Gilliam had, perhaps, his greatest season in 1963. With Sandy Koufax the No. 1 candidate for the Cy Young Award, Gilliam is the Dodgers' leaping MVP aspirant. Playing both second and third base with equal agility and producing one timely hit after another, Gilliam was the sparkplug of the club's pennant push. He had many fine games but the one which was the clincher was a great night at Candlestick September 6 when Jim made three hits, including a home run, walked once, scored four times and was robbed of a hit when he lined to second base. That splurge led the Dodgers to a 5-to-2 victory which sent the Giants tumbling into fourth place.

(Dodgers are pictured in these pages as seen by noted artist, NICHOLAS VOLPE, in his series of portraits. Our sincere thanks for their courtesy. Front Cover: By Volpe with fine aerial shot by Ralph Crane—Courtesy Life Magazine. ©1962 Time Inc.)

11

Figure 1.25. (*continued*) Page from a 1963 Los Angeles Dodgers team-signed World Series program (World Champions).

A NOTE ON TEAM-SIGNED BALLS FROM OTHER SPORTS

A number of other professional sports—including football, basketball, and soccer—also produce team-signed balls, although the practice of a team signing a ball did not arise in those sports until much later than in baseball (and in fact it might have been inspired by the prevailing practice in baseball). Those other sports collectively do not produce team balls in anywhere near the numbers signed by Major League Baseball teams, however, in part because the demand is much lower, and in part because footballs, basketballs, and soccer balls are much more expensive than baseballs. They also tend to be much less reliable media for autographs than baseballs, and they can be particularly susceptible to fading and damage from deflation over time, although certainly there are some fine examples in existence.

TWO

THE HISTORY OF TEAM BASEBALLS

When and why did team balls originate? Those are difficult questions to answer, because the practice of teams signing baseballs arose gradually. No one rang a bell and announced that it was time for baseball players to start putting pen to leather. Compounding the difficulty for the researcher, no one still living was involved in Major League baseball in the early 1910s, when team balls first began to appear. We are left to piece together the history of team balls using the testimonials of players, officials, and clubhouse workers, common sense, and perhaps the best evidence of all, the surviving baseballs themselves. The authors' research is ongoing, however, and we hope to expand this chapter in a future edition of this book.

WHEN

The earliest team balls that have come to light date from the second decade of the twentieth century. Team balls from that period are exceptionally rare, however (suggesting that very few were signed), and the majority of them seem to be from championship teams. Two of the earliest team balls known are presented in Figures 2.1 and 2.2. Figure 2.1 shows an extremely rare (and probably one-of-a-kind) team ball signed by the World Champion 1913 Philadelphia Athletics, which includes Frank "Home Run" Baker, Connie Mack, and Eddie Plank. Figure 2.2 shows a ball signed by the American League Champion 1914 Philadelphia Athletics, which came from the collection of Ferdie Moore, whose Major League career consisted

Figure 2.1. 1913 Philadelphia Athletics team ball (World Champions). Possibly the oldest complete World Championship team ball in existence.

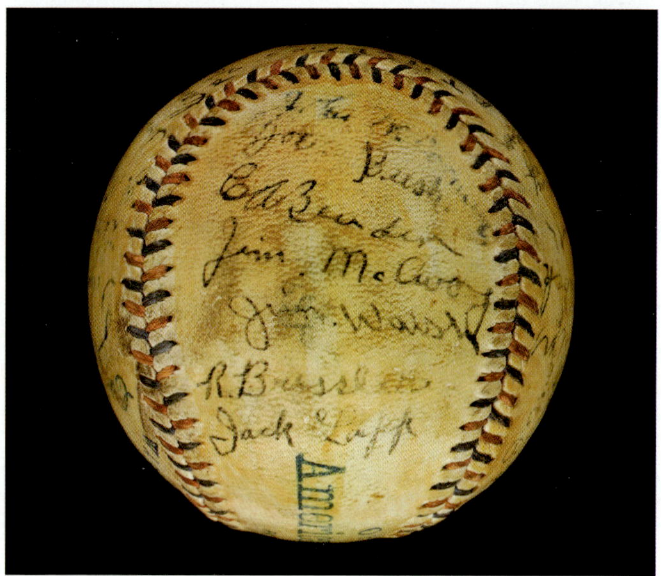

Figure 2.2. 1914 Philadelphia Athletics team ball (American League Champions).

of appearances in two games for the 1914 Athletics at the age of 18. Another example is the World Champion 1914 "Miracle" Boston Braves team ball depicted in Figure 2.3, one of two such balls donated by the family of team member Johnny Evers to the University of Notre Dame. Two team balls from the 1915 Red Sox have been sold at auction in recent years—one came from "Smoky Joe" Wood's family, and the other one might have originally belonged to Ty Cobb. Figure 2.4 shows a team ball signed by the infamous 1919 American League Champion Chicago White Sox (often referred to as the "Black Sox" because of the gambling scandal that was associated with the 1919 World Series).

Not all early team balls that have survived are from championship teams. Figure 2.5 depicts a team ball signed by the 1916 Detroit Tigers, including Ty Cobb. Note that the ball also exhibits a contemporaneous signature of legendary pitcher Walter Johnson, who, of course, pitched for the Washington Senators, indicating that it might have been signed at a game between the two teams during the 1916 season.

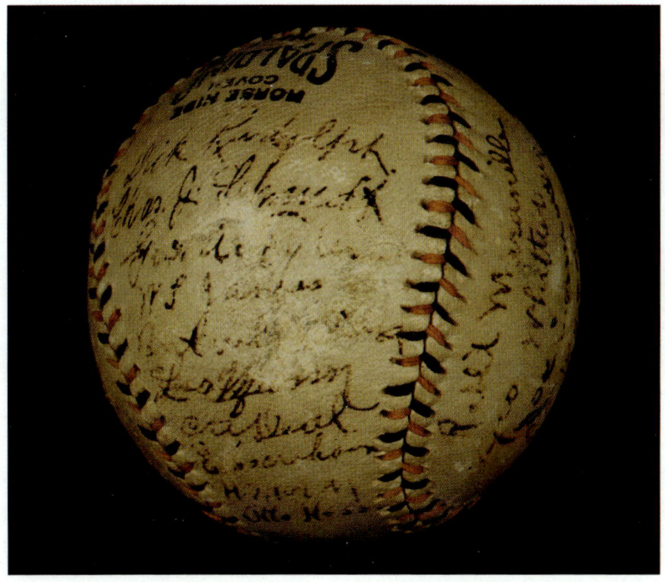

Figure 2.3. 1914 Boston Braves team ball (World Champions). (Courtesy of the Department of Special Collections of the University Libraries of Notre Dame)

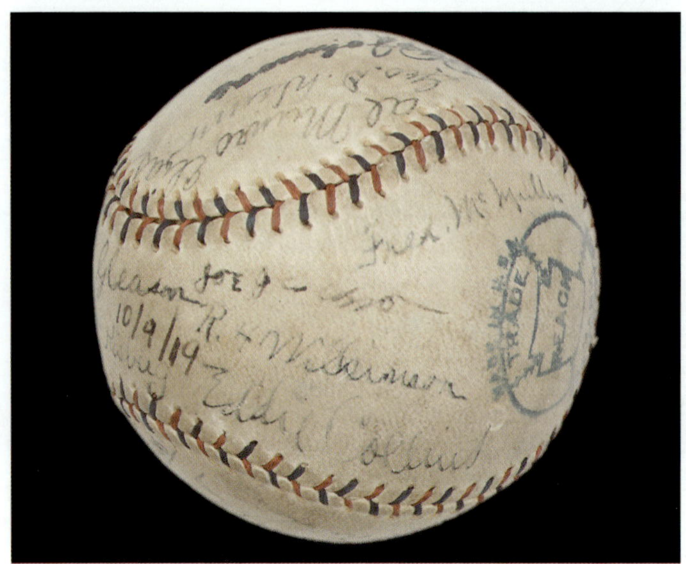

Figure 2.4. 1919 Chicago White Sox team ball (American League Champions). (Courtesy of Legendary Auctions)

Figure 2.5. 1916 Detroit Tigers team ball, one of the best-preserved early team balls in existence.

By 1920, we begin to see more team balls from a variety of Major League clubs, not just championship teams. Although very rare, team balls exist from all 1920s Major League teams, and it is likely that balls were signed sporadically, such as at the end of a season as mementos for the players. By the mid-1930s, most teams apparently included regular team ball signings in their routines. By 1939, a team ball was enough of a symbol of a team for a photograph of a 1939 Cincinnati Reds team ball to be included in an advertisement in the Reds' World Series program of that year (Figure 2.6).

By the 1940s most teams were producing team balls by the dozens. In 1998, one of the authors interviewed a man who had been a clubhouse employee and then a batboy with the Detroit Tigers organization from 1948 through 1952, including serving as a batboy at the 1951 All-Star Game held at Briggs Stadium in Detroit. In the interview he recalled that, on an average game day during his tenure, a dozen team balls were signed in the home clubhouse by the Tigers, "sometimes more, sometimes less." The number of team balls signed by the visiting teams varied and was based on the number of signed balls requested by the players themselves (usually to be given to friends) or by various dignitaries. He also recalled that "five or six dozen" team balls were signed by each team at the 1951 All-Star Game.

Figure 2.6. Pogue's department store advertisement depicting a 1939 Cincinnati Reds team ball, from the 1939 Reds World Series program.

The practice of signing significant quantities of team balls has continued to the present. Every Major League clubhouse has a table where boxes of baseballs are placed for signing by the team practically every day of the season. Players know that they are expected to take a few minutes each day to sign the balls, and most do so. It is so much a part of the daily routine of a Major League player that the 1994 film *Little Big League* includes a scene in the clubhouse in which several players are shown sitting around a table signing team balls before a game.

WHY

It might be impossible to determine definitively why the tradition of team ball signing started. There is no one living from the period when such signing began who can explain why it happened, and apparently it was not the type of phenomenon that would have inspired a written record at the time.

We are left to use the evidence that does exist, as well as inference and a little informed imagination. The authors' theory is that the practice of signing team balls owes its origin most directly to the commemorative "trophy balls" that were produced in the nineteenth century.

Beginning with the inception of the modern game of baseball itself back in the 1850s, it became customary on the amateur, collegiate, and eventually professional levels to produce a commemorative trophy ball after an important game. The actual baseball used in such a game would be carefully coated with paint or gold leaf and then calligraphically marked with information such as the names of the participating teams, the date, and the score. In that way, the ball would be preserved as a trophy for the victors to display for years to come. Many of those balls are extant; see Figure 2.7 for an example.

The trophy balls that have appeared on the market seem to be concentrated in the period from 1860 to 1890. After that time, based on the anecdotal evidence of balls that have come to market, the practice of creating elaborate trophy balls seems to have tapered off dramatically and to have disappeared completely (at least on the Major League level) by the second decade of the twentieth century.

In place of trophy balls arose the practice of signing baseballs to commemorate special events. A good historian should never fall into the trap

Figure 2.7. Trophy ball from the 1876 National League championship game between the Chicago White Stockings and the Hartford Dark Blues. (Courtesy of Legendary Auctions)

of simply assuming that, just because the end of one practice coincides with the beginning of another, there is a causal connection between the two events or that one practice was consciously replaced by the other. In this case, however, because trophy balls and team balls served the same purpose —creating a memento or artifact of a particular game or team—and the former died out approximately when the latter arose, it is reasonable to infer that team balls developed to fill the same basic purpose as trophy balls and all but replaced them.

To the authors' knowledge, no genuine autographed team balls have come to light from any time before approximately 1910, and therefore it would be reasonable to infer that there was no practice of signing such balls before that time. If there were such a practice, it is very likely that some of those balls would have survived and would have reached the market (as the trophy balls have done). Baseballs were an expensive commodity at that time; they were used sparingly in games and were not replaced until they became completely unusable. The use of perfectly good baseballs for such a seemingly trivial purpose as signing probably would have seemed absurd, if anyone had thought of it at all.

It was, however, not considered trivial at all—and in fact was well accepted and customary—to commemorate an important game by transforming a game ball into an artifact or memento of the occasion. Where previously a trophy ball had been produced, the practice arose of obtaining the signatures of players (and perhaps other dignitaries present) on a game ball. As examples, we present two balls used in the 1909 World Series between the Pittsburgh Pirates and the Detroit Tigers and signed by players. The ball shown in Figure 2.8 is inscribed to testify to its use in Game Two of the Series and is signed by numerous members of the participating teams. Figure 2.9 depicts a ball inscribed by Pirates player-manager Fred C. Clarke as having been used in Game Three of the Series and having been presented by Clarke to a Lucy Crawford.

It was that concept of having the participants in an important game sign a game ball that seems to have led directly to the modern practice of signing team balls. It was but a short step from commemorating a particular game to commemorating a particular team, especially a championship

Figure 2.8. Game-used and signed ball from Game Two of the 1909 World Series. (Courtesy of Hunt Auctions)

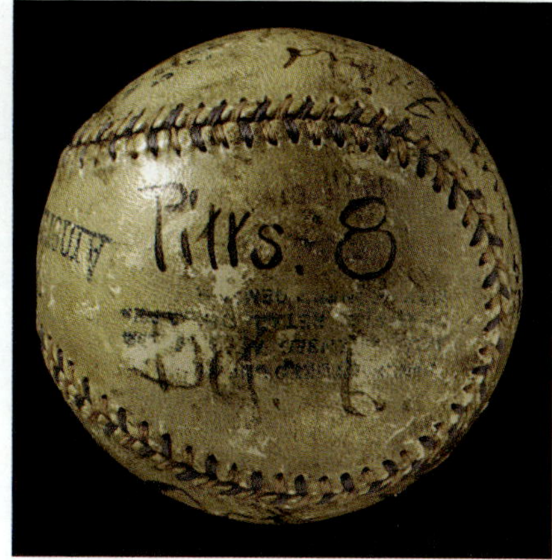

Figure 2.9. Game-used and signed ball from Game Three of the 1909 World Series. (Courtesy of Hunt Auctions)

team. As discussed previously, most of the earliest extant team balls are from championship teams. There are two possible reasons for that phenomenon: (1) that the signing of team balls began as a method of creating a memento of a successful season; and (2) that team balls from championship teams have tended to be kept and preserved by their owners more carefully than other team balls. While both reasons are probably valid, it seems reasonable to conclude that the first signings of team balls were motivated by a desire to commemorate a successful team by producing a memento of that team, which was made more personal by actually including the signatures of the team members. It was like creating a small-scale analogue of a signed historical document (such as the Mayflower Compact or the Declaration of Independence) for a baseball team—an artifact of a great team and great events. One also should not discount the effect of mass production of baseballs and the resulting lower unit price after the turn of the century; the lower price and more frequent replacement of balls during games made more baseballs available for autographs and use as mementos.

The evidence thus seems to corroborate the thesis that team balls started by commemorating special games (as had their predecessors, the trophy balls), moved rapidly to the commemoration of great teams, and ultimately became mementos of all teams. The team ball has now become an integral part of the game of baseball, and today team balls are signed not only by Major League teams but also by Olympic teams, minor league teams, college teams, and even amateur and little league teams. The team ball has become a cherished symbol of triumphs, heroes, friends, and good times past.

The authors do not intend to suggest that the trophy ball has completely died out. It is still very much with us today, albeit in a somewhat different form, and in fact in some cases it has merged with the team ball. For example, many balls are extant that were used in an important game such as a World Series game and then signed afterward by one of the participating teams. Baseballs used in no-hitters, or in other milestone games like a pitcher's 300th win, have long been kept and inscribed and signed by the pitcher involved or by an umpire. What were the scrambles for Mark McGwire and Sammy Sosa home run balls during the 1998 season, and Barry Bonds home run balls in 2001 and afterward, but quests for trophy balls? Today trophy balls and team balls exist side by side. Sometimes they are one and the same, and sometimes they are separate and distinct, but they both serve as artifacts of baseball history.

THREE

CLASSIFICATION AND AUTHENTICATION

This chapter and Chapter Four on "clubhouse" signatures are the most important chapters in this book, because authenticity is the essential issue in collecting autographs. If an autograph is not authentic, there is simply no reason for a collector to own it. This chapter addresses the classification of a team ball by year and team (part of the process of authentication) and introduces the methodology of signature authentication.

Over the last decade, the news has been full of stories of forged sports autographs.[1] The profile of the problem was certainly raised by the Federal Bureau of Investigation's undercover investigation called "Operation Bullpen," which produced 62 convictions.[2] Although entire team balls are not often forged, team balls have their own set of authenticity issues, of which a prudent collector must become knowledgeable.[3] The consequences of collecting without such knowledge can be disappointment and significant monetary loss resulting from purchasing wholly or partially non-authentic items that turn out to be worth much less than originally supposed.

Let us begin with a premise: as in the case of any autographed item, the authenticity of a team ball is a matter of opinion. Unless one personally witnesses the entire signing of the ball (which is normally impossible), one cannot state with absolute certainty that it is authentic. One can, however, establish authenticity to a practical certainty through the application of knowledge and experience.

Beginning in the late 1990s—not coincidentally the period during which Internet auctions became popular—a cottage industry of "authenticators" arose who would authenticate sports autographs for a fee. A few of them were talented and honest and have gone on to establish themselves as authorities in the industry. Yet some of those who passed themselves off as authenticators—complete with alleged law enforcement credentials, certifications from professional societies, and past appearances as expert witnesses in court proceedings—seemed to have little or no expertise or to be downright dishonest. Many plainly non-authentic autographs passed their inspection, and most of them have now been discredited, owing in part to the efforts of the FBI. The sports memorabilia market is particularly susceptible to fraud, and there is no shortage of non-authentic merchandise being peddled every day by the ignorant, the reckless, and the unscrupulous.

Reliance on an authenticator who does not have proven and widely recognized expertise in the hobby is misplaced. Collectors should rely only on established experts who can provide solid references from other savvy collectors and trustworthy dealers and auction houses, and they should develop their own ability to authenticate team balls as well. One does not have to be a "forensic expert" or a "questioned document examiner" to authenticate a team ball. In no particular order, the most important skills and assets necessary to authenticate team balls are the following: (1) familiarity with players' signatures; (2) access to a good file of examples of signatures that are reasonably believed to be authentic; (3) knowledge of factors that might indicate forgery; (4) knowledge of factors that indicate when a ball was signed (such as the age of different baseballs and the appearance of writing produced with different pens and inks); and (5) intelligence, a keen eye, experience, and common sense. All of those—with the possible exception of common sense—can be developed.

When it comes to authenticity, team ball collectors enjoy two significant advantages over collectors of single-signature balls. First, in order to forge a team ball convincingly, a forger must master the signatures of numerous persons rather than the one signature required for a single-signature ball. Creating a credible-looking forged team ball is, therefore, a very arduous, time-consuming, research-intensive process, while forging a single-signature ball is relatively quick and easy for a skilled forger.

Second, a team ball must be dated to a specific year, and thus, in order to be authentic, the baseball itself must have been manufactured during or prior to that year. If it can be demonstrated that the ball was manufactured after that year, the ball is either (1) a reunion ball (see Chapter One), (2) a compilation of signatures from a specific team and year gathered after that year,[4] or (3) a forgery. In the case of a single-signature ball, however, as long as the ball was manufactured before the death of the signer, the date of manufacture of the ball cannot be a factor in the process of authentication.[5]

In the past, those factors have kept the prevalence of team ball forgeries to a minimum. Forgers generally confined their efforts to the most valuable vintage balls. Yet it is not unheard of to find a forgery of a much less rare and valuable ball. For example, one of the authors once discovered a completely forged 1982 American League All-Star team ball, and it was masterfully done. In recent years, with the advance of prices, forgers seem to have increasingly directed their efforts to the production of team balls. For example, a number of completely forged team balls purporting to be from the New York Yankees from 1996 to the present, the 2002 California Angels, the 2004 and 2007 Boston Red Sox, and other teams have surfaced recently in Internet auctions.

Considering the tremendous number of team balls in existence, however, *it must be emphasized that the number of forgeries is very small.* A much more serious problem is what are referred to as "clubhouse signatures"—vintage "signatures" on a team ball that were signed not by the purported signer, but rather by someone associated with the team (usually a clubhouse employee, thus the origin of the term). Clubhouse signatures are the subject of Chapter Four. *It is essential for every serious team ball collector to learn about the clubhouse signature problem and how to identify such signatures.* Collecting team balls without knowledge of clubhouse signatures (or access to proper expertise) is simply inviting disaster—the result inevitably will be the acquisition of team balls that are at least partially nonauthentic and worth far less than the price paid for them.

The process of authenticating a team ball has two basic steps: classification and authentication.

STEP ONE: CLASSIFICATION

The process of authenticating a team ball begins with classifying the ball by team and year. Generally the seller will have already classified it. While most dealers and auction companies are correct in their classifications most of the time, errors are sometimes made, particularly by less experienced or less scrupulous sellers. It seems that classification errors usually have the effect of dating a ball to a year that would make it more valuable than a ball from the year in which it was actually signed. A collector should never rely solely on the seller's classification and should always go through the process of classifying a team ball independently before purchasing it, in order to confirm the seller's conclusion. As President Ronald Reagan said regarding arms-control agreements with the Soviet Union: "trust, but verify."

Use of References

Classifying a team ball requires a reference source that contains the rosters of Major League teams. Fortunately, several good databases are available without charge on the Internet. Among the best are www.baseball-reference.com,[6] which includes rosters and a wealth of statistics on teams and individual players going back to 1876, and www.baseball-almanac.com, which, in addition to rosters and statistics, also includes players' uniform numbers. It is very helpful to have an accurate list of coaches as well, but as of the date of this publication the aforementioned websites have not yet added that information. Historical lists of coaches are often (but not always) available on the official websites of Major League teams under News/Team History/All-Time Rosters.[7]

The Obscure Player Method

The most expedient way to date a team ball is to find the signature of a relatively obscure player (one who likely had a short Major League career), and then to consult a database to determine when that player was in the Major Leagues and the teams for which he played. After repeating that exercise for another relatively obscure player, the two players' records should then be cross-checked to determine the team or teams on which they played together. That process should quickly narrow the possibilities to the point that rosters can be consulted in order to reach a conclusion on the team and year of the ball.[8]

The Determinative Signature Method

A "determinative signature" is one that by itself conclusively dates a ball to a particular team and season (e.g., the signature of Frank Kellert on a Brooklyn Dodgers team ball conclusively dates the ball to the 1955 World Championship season) or at least to a very limited range of seasons. With some experience, collectors can often determine the team and the time period for a team ball very quickly by memorizing certain determinative signatures, at which point rosters can be consulted to narrow the ball down to a particular year. An experienced collector with a good roster reference should be able to classify a team ball within a few minutes.

Don't Stop There: Check *All* of the Signatures!

Once a preliminary conclusion is reached on the team and year, it is still very important to check each and every signature on the ball against the complete roster for the particular year in order to confirm that each player whose signature appears on the ball actually played for that team. One reason for going through that exercise is that occasionally one encounters an anomalous team ball that includes signatures for a particular team from two or more (usually contiguous) seasons. For lack of any other available explanation, many dealers refer to such balls as "spring training balls" (suggesting, usually based on pure conjecture, that they were signed during spring training before final cuts were made and regular season rosters were set), but such balls might simply contain signatures that were obtained by someone over a period that straddled two or more seasons. Such balls tend to be valued at a discount to "pure" team balls (those that contain only signatures from one team and one season), although there are certainly exceptions.

As an example of such an exception, there are a very small number of 1964 St. Louis Cardinals (World Championship) team balls that include the signature of Hall of Fame pitcher Steve Carlton, even though Carlton never made an official appearance in a game for the Cardinals during the 1964 season (see Figure 3.1). He was, however, called up to the Cardinals sometime in 1964 and apparently did sign team balls in the clubhouse even though he never appeared in a game.[9] His signature on a 1964 Cardinals

Figure 3.1. 1964 St. Louis Cardinals team ball (World Champions), including a pre-rookie Steve Carlton signature.

team ball, rather than indicating that the ball was signed over a period of two or more seasons (1964–1965), significantly enhances the value of the ball because it contains a pre-rookie signature of a future member of the Hall of Fame.

The same may be said of a Stan Musial signature on a 1964 Cardinals team ball. Although "Stan the Man" officially retired after the 1963 season, his signature does appear on a number of 1964 balls, apparently because he stayed on with the franchise in some capacity. His Hall of Fame status and longtime association with the Cardinals franchise enhance the appeal and value of such balls.

Another reason for checking all of the signatures against the roster is that sometimes the owner of a team ball will add signatures that had no connection with the particular team. The addition of such signatures can significantly reduce the value of a ball by compromising its "purity." As an example, a 1939 Yankees team ball, with an authentic Lou Gehrig signature no less, was once sold at auction. It was complete and in good condition, but someone had added Stan Musial's signature to the ball at some later point in time, which certainly diminished the ball's value.

It must be emphasized that a team ball can be dated only by the signatures that are on it, not by the signatures that are not on it. The fact that a particular player's signature is not on a team ball tells a collector absolutely nothing about the year of the ball, because that player might simply have not signed the ball. As discussed in Chapter One, a ball that contains the signatures of literally all members of a team is an extreme rarity; at least a few players' signatures are almost always missing from every team ball. Therefore the absence of a specific player's signature on a team ball does not mean that the ball does not date from a year in which that player played for the team. The inclusion of a specific player's signature, however, very definitely means that the ball dates from a year in which that player played for that team (with the rare exceptions noted earlier).

Checking the Baseball

The final task in the classification process is checking the possible range of dates of manufacture of the baseball itself, in order to confirm that its age is consistent with the date determined by analyzing the signatures. That task might seem relatively simple in the case of Official National and American League baseballs, but it is actually complex because the markings and their placement vary, sometimes subtly, from year to year. Dating "unofficial" balls (i.e., balls that were not made for professional use and were usually purchased in sporting goods stores) is even more difficult because of the large number of manufacturers, the variety of markings (and sometimes the absence thereof), and the lack of records.

Official Baseballs

Since the early twentieth century, Official National and American League baseballs have carried a stamp of the facsimile signature of the appropriate league president, first on the side panel of the baseball and then, beginning in 1934, on what is referred to as the "opposite sweet spot." It is therefore easy to determine the general period during which a genuine Official National or American League baseball was manufactured.

Many of the league presidents served lengthy terms, during which subtle and unsubtle changes were often made to the design of the Official Major League baseballs that bore their stamped signatures. To the experienced collector, those changes can be used to narrow the possible period of manufacture further. For example, Official American and National League baseballs had multicolored stitching from the time that team balls started to be signed around 1910 (red and blue for American League balls, red and black for National League balls) through the 1933 season, changing to only red stitching in 1934. For another example, William Harridge took office as president of the American League in 1931. Official American League baseballs began to carry his facsimile signature during the 1932 season, and the stamping (including the signature) continued to be done in blue ink. Beginning in 1953, the color of the ink used for the stamping was changed to green, and it remained so through the end of Harridge's presidency and on until 1970, when the color was changed to light blue during the presidency of Joe Cronin.[10]

Therefore, if an Official American League baseball with Harridge's stamped signature has green stamping, it was manufactured sometime between 1953 and 1958 (Cronin took over the presidency in 1959). If such a ball sports the signatures of a team from a year before or after that period, it is either a forgery or possibly a genuine team ball signed at a reunion or a later compilation. If it contains signatures from the proper period, then the features of the ball merely comport with, and thus serve as secondary confirming evidence of, the conclusion reached through dating the ball according to the signatures present.

It should be noted that the use of balls of discontinued design (or with the facsimile signature of a former league president) often overlaps with the use of newly designed balls (usually by not more than a single season), as supplies of the discontinued balls are exhausted. Thus, for example, it is not unusual to find a William Harridge American League ball with the signatures of a 1959 team, when Joe Cronin was the new league president.

Unofficial Baseballs

Many unofficial baseballs have been marketed over the years by numerous manufacturers. They vary significantly in quality, ranging from balls made with poor materials and workmanship to balls of a quality equivalent to Official Major League balls. Many teams have used (and still use) such unofficial balls for team ball signings. Still other teams have used (and still use) unofficial balls manufactured especially for the team and intended for signing, with the team's name or logo stamped on the ball; examples of such teams include the 1950s White Sox, the 1960s through 1980s Cubs, and the 1950s Tigers.

The signatures on unofficial balls are usually just as genuine as those on "official" team balls, but the lack of temporal markings and the wide variety of unofficial balls make it much more difficult to determine the date of manufacture of the ball. Certain design characteristics, such as bi-colored stitching, usually indicate an older baseball (from the 1930s or earlier), but that is often as much as the design of an unofficial ball can tell us. Much more research is needed in this area.

Two generalizations can be applied to team-signed unofficial balls. First, unofficial balls, particularly those made during the past 20 years, tend to be manufactured with inferior materials, and the signatures on them are more likely to fade or bleed over time than signatures on official balls. Second, collectors prefer Official Major League baseballs, and thus, all else being equal, the value of a team-signed unofficial baseball is discounted compared with the value of a team-signed Official baseball.

STEP TWO: AUTHENTICATION OF THE SIGNATURES

Once a team ball has been classified by team and year, the next (and most difficult) step in the authentication process is to determine whether the signatures are authentic. A good team ball authenticator employs broad familiarity with players' signatures, a comprehensive database of authentic signature exemplars, knowledge of different players' signing habits (including placement preferences when signing a team ball), knowledge of inks, experience, and even intuition in determining whether a ball is authentic.

Familiarity with baseball signatures can be achieved only by research and experience, and it takes a significant amount of time and effort. A collector should view as many balls as possible at shows, auctions, and exhibits, and in publications and friends' collections. It is also advisable to build a comprehensive file of photographs of reliable signature exemplars (especially those of Hall of Famers and other famous individuals) that can be used for comparison. Vast resources of authenticated exemplars are available in books and on the Internet, including databases of past auction results accessible on the websites of auction firms specializing in sports memorabilia.

When comparing signatures on a team ball to examples with established authenticity, one should look particularly at the formation of letters, the slant of the writing, the size of the signature (although it is possible to have equally authentic signatures that vary significantly in size, depending on the medium), and the relative size of the individual letters. If those factors match, the signatures are probably authentic, unless they have been signed by a very talented forger or clubhouse signer.

It is important to be on the lookout for shakiness or evidence of deliberateness in a signature. Authentic signatures are usually smooth and flowing, and shakiness or a deliberate style might indicate that the signature was signed by a forger attempting to copy a signature. There are, of course, shaky or deliberate signatures that are absolutely authentic, as in the case of signers who have a physical infirmity. For example, the signatures of Hall of Famer Luke Appling signed after his stroke are very shaky but nonetheless quite genuine.

It is also important to determine the type of pen used to sign the signatures. If a team ball is supposed to be from 1938 but was signed with a ballpoint pen, it must be a forgery, because ballpoint pens were not put into widespread use until approximately 1950 (unless, of course, it is a reunion ball).

CONCLUSION

The importance of a team ball collector developing classification and authentication skills, applying those skills meticulously, and knowing when and to whom to turn for expert advice cannot be overstated. Such skills and knowledge are the foundation of a meaningful and valuable collection, as well as bulwarks against disappointment and monetary loss.

A NOTE ON PROVENANCE

Some sellers might attempt to emphasize the provenance of a team ball as evidence of its authenticity. "Provenance" refers to the origin of an item, including the identity of a current or previous owner. A seller might point to the fact that a ball originated in the collection of a player, an umpire, or a team employee. Sometimes there is a story about someone who knew someone who allegedly went into the dugout or clubhouse and obtained the signatures personally.

It must be emphasized that authenticity and provenance are not the same; they are distinctly different concepts. Provenance is certainly important, and a ball's provenance might make it historically significant and even more valuable, depending on the identity and provability of previous owners (see Chapter Seven). Yet good provenance does not, per se, prove that a team ball is authentic. *Authenticity must be established by examining the ball itself.*

A team ball often comes with a story, but we all know that recollections fade over time. Every day, in courtrooms across the country, eyewitnesses to the same event give very different accounts of that event—not necessarily because some are being untruthful, but rather because human recollection is often inaccurate. Even though a seller might not be literally lying about the origin of a team ball, nonetheless his or her story might be fallacious. For example, the authors have seen hundreds of facsimile team balls (which contain rubber-stamped signatures) offered for sale in Internet auctions, often by someone claiming that a relative or friend obtained the signatures from the players personally. Perhaps that was what the seller was told by that relative or friend, or perhaps it is what the seller assumed had happened when he or she was given the ball 30, 40, or 50 years earlier, and the assumption has become a fact in the seller's mind over the years.

Even team balls that were actually obtained from credible sources such as players or team officials can be non-authentic in whole or in part. For example, a team ball obtained from a former player is just as likely to include clubhouse signatures as any other vintage ball of unknown provenance. The reason relates to how team balls are signed (see Chapter Two). It is exceedingly rare in the modern era for a player to go around and get a ball signed personally; most team balls are signed in the central signing area of a team's clubhouse, where they can be subject to clubhouse signing, and are then distributed back to the players or to others.

A collector should always make his or her own independent determination of authenticity by examining the signatures. If some or all of the signatures do not appear authentic, the origin of the ball does not make them so. The primary question should always be: "are the signatures genuine?" If they appear to be genuine, or if it is a close call, evidence of provenance can be used secondarily to lend credence to authenticity, but provenance can never be a substitute for authenticity.

A NOTE ON FACSIMILE TEAM BALLS

Beginning around 1950, baseballs filled with stamped "signatures" of entire teams began to be manufactured and sold at ballpark concession stands. The so-called "facsimile ball" was originally developed by former Major League infielder Dick Culler,[11] and facsimile balls continue to be sold at ballparks today. Figures 3.2, 3.3, and 3.4 show 1960 Pittsburgh Pirates, 1965 Los Angeles Dodgers, and 1969 New York Mets authentic team balls, respectively, alongside facsimile team balls from those teams.

Facsimile balls are constantly mistaken for genuine autographed team balls by the general public and even by some inexperienced collectors. It is not uncommon to see them offered for sale in print ads or in Internet auctions and represented as being the genuine article. Often the seller is not aware that the signatures are not authentic. The authors have personally seen hundreds of facsimile balls offered for sale as authentic team balls in Internet auctions.

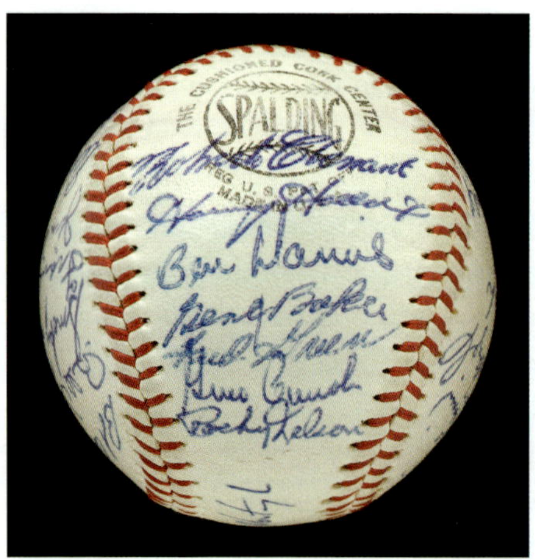

Figure 3.2. 1960 Pittsburgh Pirates authentic (left) and facsimile (right) team balls (World Champions).

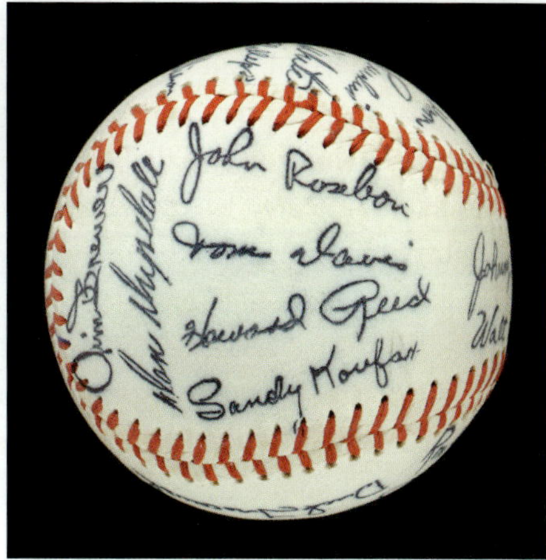

Figure 3.3. 1965 Los Angeles Dodgers authentic (left) and facsimile (right) team balls (World Champions).

Even Major League players sometimes have a problem distinguishing facsimile balls from the real thing. One of the authors once received several team balls from the early 1960s from a former player who was interested in selling them. One was a facsimile Yankees team ball (the others

Figure 3.4. 1969 New York Mets authentic (left) and facsimile (right) team balls (World Champions). Note the "Larry Berra" stamped signature on the facsimile ball fully 19 years after he began consistently signing his name "Yogi Berra" on team balls.

were authentic), and the author telephoned the player to tell him the bad news about that ball. The player was incredulous—until he received the ball back in the mail and looked at it closely. He then wrote to say that, having examined the ball closely, he agreed that it was a facsimile ball. He added that he had been deceived (he actually used another, more colorful, term) by a Yankees batboy who traded the ball to him for a genuine team ball of the National League team for which he was playing at the time. He said he had never looked at the ball closely before.

Once a collector has seen a number of authentic team balls, he or she should be able to identify a facsimile ball immediately without difficulty. A collector should particularly be on the lookout for the following factors, any of which might (but does not necessarily) indicate a facsimile ball:

1. The signatures are unusually uniform in size and color. Often there is also a slight "doubling" effect on the signatures that might be associated with rubber stamping.
2. The baseball has no trademark or other manufacturer's stamping.
3. Some or all of the signatures are randomly placed all over the ball instead of following the modern practice, according to which players sign in an organized fashion, with signatures stacked from top to bottom along the width of the panels.
4. Parts of some signatures often overlap the stitching.
5. The signatures do not touch each other. On an authentic signed team ball, the signatures, particularly descender strokes (i.e., those that descend below the normal baseline of the letters) often overlap parts of the signatures below. Because of the method by which signatures on facsimile balls are stamped, they almost never touch each other. The rare exception is a ball to which individual rubber-stamped signatures are applied; Figure 3.5 depicts such a ball that was stamped with the signatures of members of the 1946 Cardinals.
6. There are often two signatures on each of the two sweet spots (stacked one above the other). Although genuine team balls sometimes have two (and even three) signatures on the "open" sweet spot (the one without the trademark or "Official" stamp), and sometimes have a signature on the "opposite sweet

Figure 3.5. 1946 St. Louis Cardinals facsimile team ball (World Champions) with signatures individually rubber-stamped, one of the earliest facsimile balls in existence.

spot" over the stamp, they very rarely have two signatures on the opposite sweet spot.

7. Some or all of the signatures are much older (usually rookie) examples of the signatures of players whose signatures have materially changed over time. An example of that phenomenon can be clearly seen in the 1969 Mets facsimile ball shown in Figure 3.4. Yogi Berra's signature is present in the "Larry Berra" form (his real name), even though Berra had consistently signed team balls using his nickname "Yogi" starting in 1950 and continuing throughout the rest of his career (and down to the present). All genuine 1969 Mets team balls signed by Berra that the authors have seen have the "Yogi Berra" form of his signature.

Using those hints, it is often possible to identify a facsimile ball—without even seeing it—merely by asking the correct questions.

A NOTE ON RUBBER-STAMPED SIGNATURES

In very isolated cases, some teams have used rubber stamps to apply signatures to team balls. For example, Vinnie Orlando, the Red Sox equipment manager, admitted to having procured a rubber stamp of Ted Williams' signature, and the impression of that stamp can be seen on many Red Sox team balls from the late 1940s and early 1950s (Figure 3.6).[12]

The team most notorious for using rubber-stamped signatures was the New York Giants, and to a lesser extent its successor, the San Francisco Giants. The Giants' practice of stamping the manager's signature on team balls seems to have begun during Leo Durocher's tenure in the late 1940s, and it was continued by his successors Bill Rigney, Al Dark, and Herman Franks into the late 1960s, when the practice was abandoned. Certainly there are genuine managers' signatures on team balls from that era, but genuine signatures from the 1950s are very uncommon (particularly from the Durocher years, which happen to encompass the Giants' League and World

Figure 3.6. Ted Williams rubber-stamped signature on the sweet spot of a 1946 Boston Red Sox team ball (American League Champions).

Championships in 1951 and 1954, respectively). In fact, 1951 and 1954 Giants team balls are usually found with rubber-stamped Durocher signatures, with the remainder of the signatures on the ball being genuine.

Apparently the Giants also procured a rubber stamp for Hall of Famer Willie Mays, but it was seldom used. The stamp did get some use at the 1963 All-Star Game. Figure 3.7 shows a pristine 1963 National League All-Star team ball with mint, genuine signatures of the likes of Roberto Clemente, Sandy Koufax, and Duke Snider. In the midst of those genuine signatures are rubber-stamped "signatures" of Al Dark and Willie Mays. The 1963 All-Star Game was held in Cleveland, Ohio, so apparently the rubber stamps were brought to Cleveland and someone (probably a clubhouse attendant) was charged with the responsibility of stamping the balls in the clubhouse. Try to conjure up a mental picture of the great Roberto Clemente and Sandy Koufax standing in the Cleveland clubhouse signing team balls alongside a clubhouse employee wielding a couple of rubber stamps and an ink pad. The image is ludicrous.

Other cases of rubber-stamped signatures on team balls have been discovered. For example, there are some Cleveland Indians team balls from

Figure 3.7. 1963 National League All-Star team ball with rubber-stamped Willie Mays and Al Dark signatures.

the mid-1950s with a rubber-stamped signature of Manager Al Lopez. The Philadelphia Athletics of 1929–1931 also occasionally employed rubber stamps on team balls.

Rubber-stamped signatures are usually simple to identify with a trained eye. The lines of the signature are often wider than in a genuine signature, and there is often a doubling effect caused by the slight shifting of the position of the stamp during the stamping process. In addition, there are often small lines of ink residue away from the signature, caused by the edges of the stamp brushing against the round surface of the ball during stamping. The stamped signature is often (but not always) a different color from all other signatures on the ball, and the signature often has a stiff, unnatural appearance and stands out from the others. Finally, parts of the signature often overlap the stitching without any of the "skip" that would normally be caused by the pen encountering the stitches.

Some rubber-stamped signatures are very difficult to distinguish from the real thing, however, because they can resemble fountain pen signatures. One of the authors once saw a Cincinnati Reds "team ball" from approximately 1949 at a sports memorabilia show. It was a Ford Frick Official National League baseball, and it took a few minutes of close examination to determine that the signatures had been stamped. The stamped signatures had the appearance of fountain pen ink.

A NOTE ON TRACED SIGNATURES

A collector will occasionally encounter a team ball on which some or all of the signatures have been traced over by someone seeking to make the signatures appear darker. Tracing is usually found on older balls, and often it has been done by someone who innocently thought that it would enhance the ball's appearance and even its value.

The problem is that a ball with traced signatures is at best worth only a fraction of what it would have been worth absent the tracing, even though the untraced signatures might have been worn or faded. Most collectors treat such a ball as being non-authentic and would not consider the ball to be collectible at all for that reason.

One of the authors was once shown photographs of a 1918 Red Sox team ball with the signature of a young Babe Ruth, which unfortunately had been traced over at some point by a member of the family of the original owner, who had been a member of that team. The tracing reduced a ball that could have had value well into five figures to one with highly uncertain (but certainly significantly lower) value.

Tracing can be very difficult to spot, especially when it was done many years ago with vintage writing instruments. A collector should particularly be on the lookout for the following factors, any of which might (but does not necessarily) indicate traced signatures:

1. The signatures on a vintage team ball are especially bold and vibrant, to the point of appearing unnatural. That is certainly not to say that all (or even most) vintage balls with bold signatures are traced. There are many specimens of vintage team balls that have survived in pristine condition without any enhancement. Yet unnaturally bold signatures should at least raise suspicion and prompt closer inspection. That suspicion should be even greater when the boldness of the signatures on a ball varies significantly.
2. There appear to be divergences between the lines of some of the letters in some of the signatures; the lines of the older, faded signature are sometimes visible under or next to the lines of the superimposed traced signature. It is helpful to view the signatures under magnification in order to spot such divergences. The exception is that, very rarely, one will encounter a portion of a signature that was traced over by the original signer contemporaneously with the original signing of the ball, because the pen did not write well on the first attempt. Such a signature should be considered authentic.
3. More than one color of ink is present in a signature. The exception is that, very rarely, one will encounter a signature that is authentically signed in two different colors of ink because the signer had difficulty with the first pen. Such a signature should be considered authentic.
4. One or more of the characteristics of forgery are present. Remember that traced signatures are essentially forgeries superimposed over genuine signatures, so, for example, evidence of deliberateness might indicate the presence of tracing. Similarly, if the type of pen or ink used was not available

when the ball was supposed to have been signed, that factor might also indicate tracing.

Notes

1. For lack of a better word, the term "forgery" (and related terms) will be used in this book to refer to a team ball created (often, but not always, a significant period of time after the purported year of the ball) with the intent to pass it off as an authentic item and thus profit from the transaction. The use of the term here does not conform to the strict legal meaning of "forgery" or the crime of "forgery."

2. See http://www.fbi.gov/hq/cid/fc/ec/sm/smoverview.htm. See also Kevin Nelson, *Operation Bullpen* (Southampton Books, 2006). Operation Bullpen followed on the heels of Operation Foul Ball, a sports memorabilia fraud investigation conducted during the mid-1990s by the Chicago Division of the FBI. That operation resulted in the conviction of 14 individuals in five states involved with forging and distributing forged memorabilia.

3. The incidence of entirely forged team balls being offered for sale has been increasing over the last few years, however, particularly in Internet auctions. Most of those balls are very poor forgeries of team balls of recent teams such as the Braves and Yankees. It seems that the forgers are attempting to take advantage of the poor (or rushed) penmanship of many modern players, as well as the supposed lack of knowledge of many Internet bidders.

4. This method of assembling a team ball has traditionally been uncommon, because the effort and expense of obtaining a team ball in this manner would almost always exceed the value of the finished product. Therefore someone who desires a team ball from a particular team will usually just purchase one. Some collectors, however, prefer the experience of creating a team ball by personally obtaining the signatures of a favorite team gradually over time. Recently some dealers have begun to assemble team balls by obtaining signatures in airports and hotel lobbies and at stadiums—a practice that often results in a ball full of hurried signatures.

5. There is an exception to that rule, for players whose signatures change over time. In that case it might be possible to show temporal incongruity between the ball and the style of the signature; the style of the signature might be such that it could not have been signed on the particular ball because of the date of the ball's manufacture.

6. At the time of publication, www.baseball-reference.com is offering, at no charge, downloads of the all-time player statistics in Adobe format; see http://www.baseball-reference.com/blog/the-baseball-reference-player-folio-on-your-e-reader. Those files were built using the data at www.baseball-databank.org.

7. See, for example, http://chicago.cubs.mlb.com/chc/history/coaches.jsp. It should be kept in mind that such lists are often works in progress and can be incomplete.

8. At the time of publication of this book, James Spence Authentication is planning to add to its website (www.spenceloa.com) a link to a database that will enable a visitor to apply the obscure player method automatically by inputting the names of several players from a team ball.

9. Carlton was issued a Cardinals uniform in 1964, proving that he was called up from one of his minor league teams at some point, probably late in the season. See Mark Stang and Linda Harkness, *Baseball by the Numbers* (Lanham, Md.: Scarecrow Press, 1997), 1084. Because he was issued number 32, he must have been called up after June 15, 1964, because Ernie Broglio, who previously wore that number, was traded by the Cardinals to the Cubs on that day in a multi-player trade that brought Lou Brock to the Cardinals. A book such as *Baseball by the Numbers,* which lists all uniform numbers issued in a season, can be very helpful in explaining the appearance of the signature of a player who did not actually appear in a game. *Baseball by the Numbers* also includes coaches.

10. Official American League baseballs from the early 1960s with blue stamping are known to exist, although they are very uncommon. The authors believe that they are genuine, but they are not aware of any explanation for the aberrant color.

11. Robert W. Creamer, "Hey Mister, Can We Have Your Autograph?," *Sports Illustrated,* April 12, 1982, 108.

12. *Boston Globe,* August 7, 1995, 45.

FOUR

CLUBHOUSE SIGNATURES

The most significant peril facing a team ball collector in purchasing a ball is the "clubhouse signature." A clubhouse signature is a non-authentic signature of a player, manager, or coach that was applied to a team ball by someone associated with the team contemporaneously with the season during which the ball appears to have been signed. Clubhouse signatures were usually signed by a member of the clubhouse staff (thus the origin of the term), but some might have been signed by other team personnel or even other players.

The term "clubhouse signature" is distinguished from what is referred to as a "forgery" in common parlance merely by the identity and status of the person who applied the signature, the time at which it was signed, and perhaps the tolerance or express authorization of the person whose name was signed.[1] The difference is, however, purely semantic—a clubhouse signature is just as non-authentic as a forgery. The term "clubhouse" corresponds to the term "secretarial," which is used to describe signatures applied by a secretary to letters or other manuscripts.[2] Unlike forgeries, and like secretarial manuscript signatures, clubhouse signatures were often expressly or tacitly authorized, or at least tolerated, by the person whose name was being signed.

The existence of clubhouse signatures is generally known among team ball collectors and dealers. Yet despite the growing comprehension of the problem in recent years, its full extent is still not widely recognized. The purpose of this chapter is to illuminate the scope of the problem and arm the reader with the tools necessary to identify and avoid clubhouse signatures. The information presented here is based on many years of intensive research by the authors, including the viewing of tens of thousands of team balls.

There has been very little attempt in hobby literature to identify clubhouse signature problems. The only way for the team ball market to mature and grow, however, and the only way to build collector confidence, is to raise the level of knowledge in the marketplace—among dealers and collectors alike. Only a decade ago many people seemed to be in denial regarding the extent of the clubhouse signature problem. Fortunately, the problem is now out in the open, where it should continue to be discussed and debated openly and honestly. The increasing use by sellers of qualified third-party authenticators—who are constantly improving their ability to identify clubhouse signatures and noting them in their letters of authenticity (see Chapter Five)—has certainly helped to raise awareness.

THE SCOPE OF THE PROBLEM

It is possible to find clubhouse signatures on team balls from every team, and from the dawn of the practice of signing team balls through the present day. The problem is very serious—the authors have personally seen thousands of team balls with one or more clubhouse signatures. The seriousness is compounded by the fact that a few of the clubhouse signers were masters at their craft, sometimes fooling even some of today's experts.

Usually, a ball with clubhouse signatures will contain only one or perhaps a few such signatures, with the remainder of the signatures on the ball being authentic. There are some instances in which *entire* team balls are composed of clubhouse signatures.

The incidence of clubhouse signatures should not come as a surprise to those who have followed the many disclosures of the practice in the media in the recent past. Perhaps the most famous revelation occurred during Ted Williams' February 1996 interview with Morley Safer of CBS's *60 Minutes*. Asked whether someone ever signed for him during his playing days, Williams responded: "Yeah, . . . the clubhouse boy could sign my name like gangbusters. Yes, sir. And not only me, a lot of the members of the team. He had them all down pretty good." He added: "[There are] a lot of autographs out there that have been signed by the bat boy and the secretary and all the rest of them."[3]

Other such disclosures abound. In the wake of Williams' revelation, former Yankee Hank Bauer confirmed that, during his playing career from 1947 to 1961, "[clubhouse boys] would sign for the star players." He added, however, that he signed the "eight dozen baseballs a day" himself because he "had pretty good handwriting" and "they couldn't duplicate it."[4] In 1996, Chicago news anchor Walter Jacobson admitted in an interview that as a young Cubs batboy he had forged players' signatures on baseballs, adding "I could write Hank Sauer's name now so you couldn't tell the difference."[5] Former Cincinnati Reds and Minnesota Twins batboy Randall Marshall admitted to having forged players' signatures in a 1998 interview with HBO's Jim Lampley.[6]

Joe Carriera, a New York attorney who worked as a Yankees batboy from 1949 to 1955, has recalled that "longtime [Yankees] clubhouse manager Pete Sheehy 'did Joe DiMaggio better than Joe; Joe was too busy and didn't want to be bothered.'"[7] Another ex-Yankees batboy, Joe D'Ambrosio, has admitted to having forged Yogi Berra, Reggie Jackson, and Billy Martin signatures in the Yankees clubhouse during the 1970s. D'Ambrosio bluntly alluded to the scope of the problem in terms that should send a chill down the spine of every collector: "Every team has a guy like me."[8] A man who served as a batboy for the Detroit Tigers from 1948 to 1952 recalled in a 1998 interview with one of the authors that, during his tenure, a man who he described as a "stadium usher" was seen signing entire Tigers team balls in a room adjacent to the clubhouse. In a 2007 interview, Bill Malone, a former clubhouse manager for the Cleveland Indians in the 1960s, admitted signing the names of manager Birdie Tebbetts and other players on team balls, and added that "I know some of the teams where not only the clubbie would sign the names but some had a player who was expert at signing most of the other guys names."[9]

If additional evidence of the magnitude of the clubhouse signature phenomenon is desired, one need only speak directly with former Major League players, coaches, and clubhouse staff. Many of them readily acknowledge the existence of clubhouse signers, although some are reluctant to discuss the subject publicly, to be quoted, or to name the clubhouse signers or the players whose names were signed. The problem has also received some attention in hobby publications.[10]

One point must be made crystal clear: considering the tremendous number of team balls that have been signed over the years, *the vast majority of signatures on team balls are genuine.* The clubhouse signature problem is most prevalent with respect to the signatures of certain players during certain time periods. That said, however, the clubhouse signature problem has existed for many years and remains to this day.[11] The problem primarily affects managers and star players, but clubhouse signatures of common players are not uncommon.

THE 1939 LOU GEHRIG EXAMPLE

One relatively well-known and widely acknowledged example of the clubhouse signature phenomenon is the prevalence of Lou Gehrig clubhouse signatures on 1939 Yankees team balls. Every baseball fan, and everyone who has seen the film *Pride of the Yankees,* knows the tragic story of how an ailing Lou Gehrig removed himself from the Yankees lineup in 1939 after appearing in only eight games, never to return. Someone in the clubhouse continued to apply his name sporadically to 1939 team balls for the rest of the season, however, apparently out of respect for "The Iron Horse."

A 1939 Yankees team ball with a genuine Lou Gehrig signature (and there are a small number of examples in existence) commands a tremendous price premium over a ball with a clubhouse signature. For an experienced collector, a clubhouse Lou Gehrig signature is usually fairly simple to identify as such. Figure 4.1 depicts an example of a clubhouse Gehrig signature on a 1939 Yankees team ball, and Figure 4.2 depicts genuine Gehrig signatures from 1939 and earlier Yankees team balls. The formation of many of the letters in the 1939 clubhouse signature is markedly different from the formation of the same letters in the authentic examples, which are very consistent (allowing for the natural evolution of Gehrig's signature over time); in the clubhouse signature the first and last names are not connected (as they are in the authentic versions), the rise of the ascender in the *h* is exaggerated, and the capital *L* and *G* are grossly misformed.

OTHER CASE STUDIES

It is well beyond the scope of this book to conduct an exhaustive survey of clubhouse signature problems. Instead, the authors have opted to present several illustrated case studies in order to alert collectors to the problem

Figure 4.1. Clubhouse Lou Gehrig signature (1939).

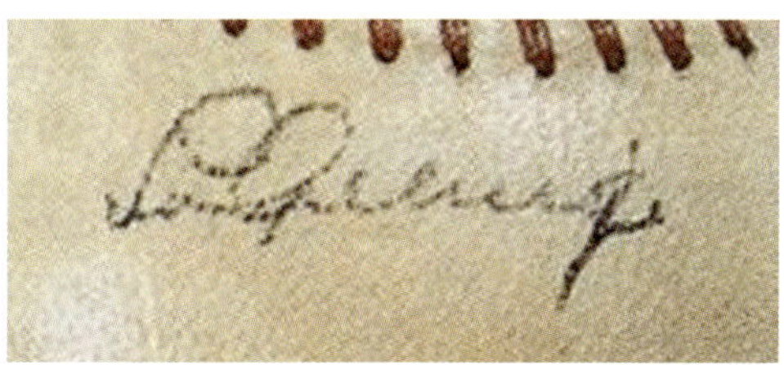

Figure 4.2. Authentic Lou Gehrig signatures (from top): 1936, 1937, and 1939. The 1939 example was signed by Gehrig at the 1939 World Series, and it is undoubtedly among the last signatures that he signed on a baseball.

and to illustrate the methodology involved in identifying clubhouse signatures. Ultimately, the best way to avoid purchasing balls with clubhouse signatures is to learn the authentication methods discussed in Chapter Three and to gain experience by viewing as many team balls as possible.

When it comes to clubhouse signatures, or authenticity in general, the best advice is to take the principle of *caveat emptor* ("let the buyer beware") very seriously. Many dealers, particularly those who only dabble in team balls on a limited basis, have little or no knowledge of the clubhouse signature phenomenon, and even if they are aware of the problem they might not be skilled at identifying clubhouse signatures. Therefore, collectors should always be prepared to protect their own interests and to seek expert advice when necessary.

Case Study One: Mickey Mantle

It should be well known that there are many Yankees team balls with clubhouse signatures of Mickey Mantle. After all, former Yankees pitcher Jim Bouton discussed the issue very frankly in his famous book *Ball Four*:

> I don't like the Mantle that refused to sign baseballs in the clubhouse before the games. Everybody else had to sign, but Little Pete [Previte] forged Mantle's signature. So there are thousands of baseballs around the country that have been signed not by Mickey Mantle, but by Pete Previte.[12]

Where are those thousands of Yankees team balls? They are out there somewhere. It would be the height of foolishness to believe that only the team balls with genuine Mantle signatures have survived and are reaching the market. Not only would it be foolish, it would be patently untrue. Yankees team balls with clubhouse Mantle signatures are sold all the time to unsuspecting collectors, although much less frequently as the understanding of the problem and the use of expert authenticators has grown in recent years.

Distinguishing between genuine and clubhouse Mantle signatures is complicated by the fact that his signature changed significantly from the time that he came to the Major Leagues as a 19-year-old rookie in 1951 to the time that he retired after the 1968 season. For ease of reference, the left column of Figure 4.3 contains year-by-year examples of Mickey Mantle signatures taken from Yankees or All-Star team balls, which, in the authors' opinion, are authentic. Although the signatures obviously change over time, one can readily see the evolution. In the right column, the most prevalent examples of what the authors believe to be clubhouse signatures from team balls are shown. With such a side-by-side comparison, one can readily see the differences and the scope of the problem.

The authors have conducted an intensive study of Mickey Mantle signatures. The general findings (admittedly anecdotal) can be summarized as follows. First, nearly all Mantle signatures on team balls from 1951 through 1954 are genuine. The authors have seen exceptions on a handful of team balls from that period, but they are usually obvious forgeries, which should be detected readily by experienced collectors. Clubhouse Mantle signatures start appearing in significant numbers in 1955 (although in that year they are still the exception) and become more and more prevalent as time goes on. The authors estimate that roughly 10–15% of Mantle signatures on 1955 Yankees team balls are clubhouse signatures, with that number rising to roughly 20–25% in 1956, jumping to 80% in 1957, and reaching 90% or more from 1958 through Mantle's retirement in 1968. Those are obviously alarming numbers. By the early 1960s, it is extremely rare to find an authentic Mantle signature on a Yankees team ball.

It should be noted that nearly all Mantle signatures on All-Star team balls throughout his career are genuine, even in the later years. He was apparently willing to take the time to sign on those special occasions, when the balls were going to be distributed to his teammates and to umpires and league officials. A more practical reason might have been that his clubhouse signer was usually not available at All-Star Games.

The purpose of this discussion is not to pick on Mickey Mantle, who was obviously one of the greatest players in the history of the game, and for whom the authors have great respect. He had responsibilities to the press and the public that many others never had, and the demands on his time were thus much greater than average (although other stars of the 1950s and 1960s found the time to sign team balls, as do many contemporary stars). It should also be noted that the practice of using clubhouse signers had been accepted in locker rooms for as long as 30 years by the time that Mantle came to the Major Leagues, and the Yankees had been some of the most active practitioners during that time.

The purpose here is to raise the level of knowledge in the marketplace. In the future, when the purchase of a Yankees team ball from the Mantle era is being considered, the Mantle signature should be carefully inspected and authenticated. Otherwise, a collector might end up owning a ball worth significantly less than he or she paid.

Figure 4.3. Mickey Mantle: year-by-year comparison of authentic and clubhouse signatures on team balls (1951–1968).

YEAR	AUTHENTIC	CLUBHOUSE
1960		
1961		
1962		
1963		
1964		
1965		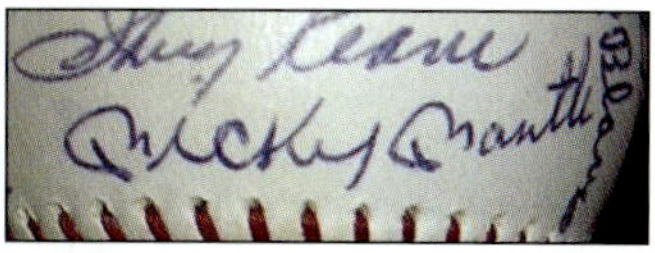
1966		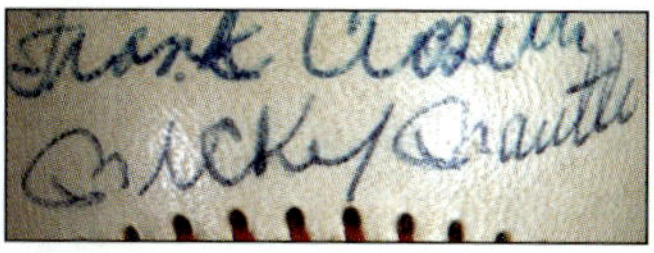
1967		
1968	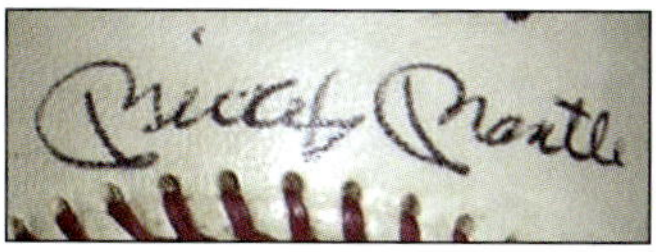	

Two different market prices for Yankees team balls from the Mantle era have developed: one price for balls with an authentic Mantle signature, which command a significant premium, and another much lower price for balls with a clubhouse Mantle signature, which still have value because of the other signatures. That same two-tiered pricing structure should ultimately be applicable to all team balls in situations in which clubhouse signatures of one or more key players are prevalent.

Case Study Two: The Brooklyn Dodgers (or, "Sign Da Balls!")

Generally, even when a clubhouse signature problem exists with respect to a certain team from a certain era, it is confined to a few star players. In the case of the Brooklyn Dodgers from the late 1940s until their move to Los Angeles in 1958, however, in some cases entire team balls were forged by a clubhouse employee: Charlie "The Brow" DiGiovanna.

Duke Snider made a point of mentioning DiGiovanna's skill as a team ball forger in his autobiography, *The Duke of Flatbush*:

> The Brow, a man in his 20s like most of us, got his name from his thick, dark, bushy eyebrows. He was a man to be reckoned with. In addition to being an efficient batboy, he had influence in other important pursuits. He could . . . sign your autograph better than you could. Sometimes The Brow would sign team balls for us. . . . *The Brow signed a lot of them—for all 25 players, the coaches, and the manager.*[13]

Another former Dodger, Rex Barney, confirmed that "[Charlie the Brow] could autograph a whole Dodger ball by himself and you would never know it from the real thing. . . . I would defy anybody to say it wasn't real."[14]

The actual team ball signing process that prevailed in the Dodgers clubhouse of the 1950s was described in a 1982 *Sports Illustrated* article:

> The Brow would prowl the clubhouse, yelling, "Sign da balls, sign da balls!" and shrug off the genial obscenities hurled at him by recalcitrant players. When he had to supply the signatures himself, it was an amazing thing to watch. He'd sit down and rapidly reproduce signature after signature, each astonishingly similar to the original, no matter how the originals varied from one another.[15]

Thus, the evidence is overwhelming that many Brooklyn Dodgers team balls produced from the late 1940s through the late 1950s contain clubhouse signatures, and that some are composed entirely of clubhouse signatures.[16] Again, it would be foolish (and incorrect) to believe that only the authentic balls have survived and are reaching the market. With Dodgers team balls from that era often routinely selling for four-figure prices and more, it is vital that collectors and dealers develop the ability to distinguish the genuine articles from the clubhouse balls.

Figure 4.4 shows genuine Jackie Robinson and Roy Campanella signatures on a 1955 Dodgers team ball, alongside clubhouse versions from the same year. It is difficult to detect the clubhouse signature in the case of Robinson, but it is somewhat easier to do in the case of Campanella, who had a more elaborate signature.

Whoever is responsible for the clubhouse signatures on Dodgers team balls from the 1940s and 1950s (and it appears to have been primarily DiGiovanna), he was a master duplicator of others' signatures. It is very difficult to identify his handiwork. Many people cannot distinguish his "signatures" from the real things.

One rule of thumb that can be offered is to avoid Dodgers team balls from the mid-1950s that feature Robinson, Campanella, and Carl Erskine

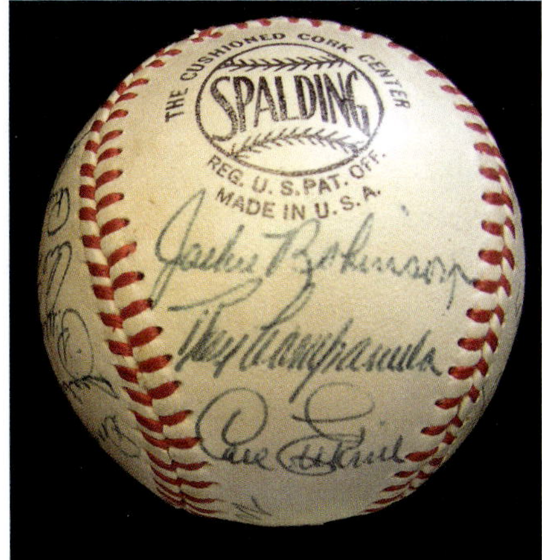

Figure 4.4. Authentic Jackie Robinson and Roy Campanella signatures from a 1955 Brooklyn Dodgers World Championship team ball (left); clubhouse Robinson and Campanella signatures from 1955 (right).

(in that order, from top to bottom) underneath the Spalding logo on an Official National League ball (see Figure 4.4).[17] That was the clubhouse signer's usual pattern. Just because a ball does not have that pattern certainly does not mean that it is free of clubhouse signatures, and just because a ball exhibits that pattern does not mean that it is definitely a clubhouse ball (although the authors have never seen a ball with that pattern that was not a clubhouse ball). One should also bear in mind that there are many Dodgers team balls from the period that have a mixture of genuine and clubhouse signatures, so it is necessary to be very careful; just because some signatures are genuine does not mean that all are genuine.

In 1958, the Dodgers' extensive clubhouse signature problem seems to have substantially ceased. Most Dodgers team balls signed after 1957 are totally genuine. In fact, the authors have seen very few clubhouse signatures on Dodgers team balls from the 1960s. Perhaps not coincidentally, Charlie DiGiovanna died of a heart attack (at the age of 27) shortly after making the move to Los Angeles with the team in 1958.[18]

Case Study Three: Ted Williams

What about Ted Williams? The bad news for collectors is that Ted's memory was still very sharp in that 1996 *60 Minutes* interview—there are indeed a substantial number of Red Sox team balls with rather convincing clubhouse Ted Williams signatures. Apparently many were signed by Vinnie Orlando, the former Red Sox equipment manager who worked in the Red Sox clubhouse for almost 50 years.[19] The good news is that Williams did, in fact, sign many team balls personally during his lengthy career.

Figure 4.5 shows five Ted Williams signatures, from different years spaced throughout his long playing career, which are genuine in the authors' opinion. Although Williams' signature changed somewhat over time, many similarities can be seen: (1) the top loop in the *T*; (2) the "figure eight" at the bottom of the *T*; (3) the separation of the *T* from the *ed*; and (4) the tendency of the top of the second *l* in the last name to be higher than the first *l*. As can be seen in the 1958 and 1960 examples, sometime in the mid-1950s Williams began connecting the *d* in his first name to the *W* in his last name. A clubhouse version of Williams' signature from 1955 is shown in Figure 4.5 for comparison.

Figure 4.5. (From top) Authentic Ted Williams signatures from 1940, 1946, 1954, 1958, and 1960. (Bottom) Clubhouse Ted Williams signature from 1955.

EFFECT ON VALUE

It is the authors' opinion that a clubhouse signature is not more valuable than a modern forged signature. It is simply not the signature of the player that it purports to be.

If a collector believed that he had Mickey Mantle's genuine signature on the sweet spot of his 1956 World Champion Yankees team ball (Mantle's

Triple Crown and Most Valuable Player year), but the signature turned out to be non-authentic, does it make him feel any better that it was signed by a Yankees clubhouse employee in 1956 rather than by a random autograph forger last month? It should not. At the risk of stating the obvious, the value of a team ball is based solely on the desirability of possessing the authentic signatures of the members of a certain team on a baseball, and if those signatures were signed by a third party—*any* third party—that value simply does not exist.

Does a team ball on which some, but not all, of the signatures are clubhouse have any value? The answer is yes, but that value is certainly diminished as compared with a completely authentic ball, and it depends heavily on the specific identities of the respective clubhouse and authentic signatures. If some of the key signatures are clubhouse signatures, then the diminution in value is greater than if the clubhouse signatures are those of common players. A team ball with a clubhouse key signature is certainly not worth any more than an otherwise identical ball that is missing that player's signature entirely, and it might be worth even less to a collector for whom the presence of any clubhouse signature taints the entire ball.

WAS IT WRONG?

Some might argue that, since team balls did not have substantial monetary value until the 1980s, when the market began to develop in earnest, the players who employed or tolerated clubhouse signers prior to that time, and the clubhouse signers themselves, really were not doing anything wrong. Ted Williams essentially made that point in his *60 Minutes* interview when, referring to clubhouse signatures, he said "it wasn't important then."[20] Former Brooklyn Dodger Rex Barney, when asked in 1995 if his teammates thought there was anything wrong with having a clubhouse employee sign autographs for them, responded similarly: "No. . . . It was just a way of life. Autographing wasn't such a big thing then."[21] The lack of monetary value associated with autographs in times past is often cited as the main reason why clubhouse signers were not engaging in wrongful behavior.[22]

It is certainly possible to take issue with the premise of that argument, which is that there was no value placed on team balls prior to the development of the sports memorabilia industry in the 1970s. Certainly we know that there was no semblance of an organized market until that time. There was, however, a "value" placed on team balls before the industry arose, simply because people obviously wanted them. It might be true that team balls did not have established monetary value until at least the 1970s, but it would be naive to assume that team balls were not previously sold or bartered for goods, services, or various other favors. In fact, there is definitive evidence that autographed baseballs were sold as early as the 1930s, and possibly substantially earlier.[23] It is reasonable to assume that someone was deriving some benefit from the distribution of team balls to the public, even if that benefit was not cold hard cash.

For present purposes, however, let us presume that the premise of the argument is correct, that team balls had no monetary value and were given away without any quid pro quo whatsoever. In that case, it can be argued that it might not be fair to judge the practices of a past era by the moral and ethical standards of today, and that it might be inappropriate to fault the past practitioners of clubhouse signing for not being prescient enough to foresee the future development of a market for team balls.[24] Nonetheless, despite those arguments, the clubhouse signers, and in some cases the players by complicity, were certainly engaged in an act of deception.

The object of clubhouse signing was obviously (and admittedly) to deceive the recipients of the autographs into believing that they had obtained genuine signatures. If the object had been otherwise, the clubhouse signers would not have made such blatant efforts to imitate the players' actual signatures. Everyone involved, including the players, the clubhouse signers, and the team front office staff, knew that the balls would be represented as authentic team-signed balls when they were given to the ultimate recipients. The fact that the motivation for the deception might not have been direct monetary gain does not negate the existence of the deception. In the authors' opinion, it is morally indefensible to take the view that, if the recipient of an autographed item did not pay cash for it, the team or player that provided the item was entitled to deceive the recipient with impunity as to the item's authenticity. Duke Snider, in his autobiography, introduced a statement regarding entire Brooklyn Dodgers team balls having been signed by "The Brow" with the phrase: "I don't want to disillusion any fans who might have baseballs autographed by the Dodger team in those years, but. . . ."[25] Disillusionment is the child of deception.[26]

Regardless of whether team balls with clubhouse signatures were ever sold or bartered, they were obviously produced for a purpose. That purpose might have been simply to serve as gifts to create goodwill among the recipients, who included friends, relatives, public officials, charities, vendors, corporate sponsors, league officials, and front office workers. That goodwill would not have been engendered if the recipients had known that they were receiving non-authentic signatures (in fact quite the contrary). After all, the recipients could have accomplished the same thing by buying a baseball and signing the players' names on it themselves. The deception is quite apparent. If the demand for team balls was greater than the supply that could be produced because of time constraints, the solution should have been to be honest and give away fewer balls.

It is important to put past clubhouse signing in context. The Major League clubhouse was (and still is) its own world, in which a culture of strict give-and-take prevails. Players were pressed for time, and clubhouse employees were responsible for getting team balls signed. Clubhouse employees were very important to players because they took care of a variety of the players' needs, and maintaining their goodwill was important, as it is to this day. From Jim Bouton, we also know that the Major League clubhouse (at least in the past) was a place where conformity was strongly encouraged, and where "rocking the boat" could endanger one's career. It was also, and remains today, an "inner sanctum" that was off limits to all but players and specific team personnel, which meant that the deception could be easily hidden.

It is easy to see how a practice like clubhouse signing might develop and be tolerated in that environment, although that certainly does not make it right. Some of the players might have harbored silent anxieties about the practice (as Bouton obviously did), but it was just not worth making an issue of it. Players were concentrating on their performance on the field and their tenure with the club; to them, signing team balls probably ranked about as high in importance in their daily routine as tying their shoes. It just was not important; it was a chore. At the same time, the clubhouse employees were charged with the task of obtaining team balls for use by the club as gifts for VIPs and others, and there is evidence that front offices were demanding and not always concerned with the authenticity of the signatures.[27] When the players' recalcitrance or lack of availability clashed with the clubhouse employees' job responsibilities, the creative solution found by the employees was often clubhouse signatures. There is also evidence that some star players actually paid clubhouse staff to sign team balls for them.[28]

Regardless of which side of the morality argument one takes, it has been clear for at least 20 years that a strong market for team balls has developed. Therefore, there can be absolutely no justification for any clubhouse signing activities taking place today, and Major League teams should be vigilant in ensuring that no forged autographs of any kind are being produced within their organizations. Today's teams seem to take that responsibility seriously,[29] but clubhouse signing is a very difficult thing to police.

As to vintage team balls, what's done is done. Those with clubhouse signatures have been scattered to the winds and frequently reach the market. We should be grateful to Rex Barney, Jim Bouton, Duke Snider, Ted Williams, and others who have come forward and told the truth about clubhouse signing. Now it is left to collectors and dealers alike to deal with the situation open-mindedly, honestly, and fairly. Collectors should remember that clubhouse signatures are the exception and should certainly not let the phenomenon interfere with their enjoyment of collecting team balls. Developing a healthy awareness of the problem is, however, prudent and indeed necessary to avoid paying full price for team balls with non-authentic signatures.

HELPFUL HINTS

The preceding examples are some of the most significant clubhouse signature problems, from the standpoints of prevalence and effect on value. As stated earlier, however, one can find clubhouse signatures on team balls from all teams and from many different time periods. The authors have seen clubhouse Warren Spahn signatures on 1950s Braves team balls, clubhouse Frank Robinson signatures on Orioles balls of the late 1960s and early 1970s, clubhouse Babe Ruth signatures on Yankees balls of the 1920s and 1930s, clubhouse Bill Dickey and Lefty Gomez signatures on Yankees balls of the late 1930s and 1940s, and clubhouse Billy Martin signatures on Yankees balls of the late 1970s (particularly 1977). There are many more examples.

While a few clubhouse signers were master forgers, most were not. Therefore, comparing suspect signatures with known authentic exemplars is often a very effective method of identifying clubhouse signatures.

One indication of possible clubhouse signing is the existence of signatures signed in different colors or shades of ink on a team ball. The reason is that, as already discussed, clubhouse signers often were engaged in filling in missing signatures after most players had already signed a ball, and frequently would use a different pen. For the same reason, one often finds clubhouse signatures in less-preferred locations on a ball, including at the very bottom or top of a panel (undesirable locations because of the cramped space). It must be emphasized, however, that neither ink color nor placement is conclusive evidence of a clubhouse signature. The vast majority of signatures in differing inks or in less-preferred locations on team balls are authentic; the point is that such signatures deserve heightened scrutiny, especially if they have both characteristics.

When there is one clubhouse signature on a ball, the chances are greater that there are more. Sometimes a clubhouse signer only signed the name of one player on team balls. Yankees team balls from the 1950s and 1960s are good examples, on which a clubhouse Mickey Mantle signature was frequently the only clubhouse signature. Often, however, clubhouse signers took on the task of "filling in" names on a team ball in order to complete them after they had obtained as many genuine signatures as time and players' willingness to sign would permit. Therefore, if one can identify one clubhouse signature, that means a clubhouse signer had contact with the ball, and thus the probability of finding additional clubhouse signatures on that ball increases. Oddly enough, sometimes one finds authentic and clubhouse versions of a player's signature on a single team ball.

As always, knowledge and experience are one's best protection when evaluating team balls. A collector should use the authentication techniques discussed in Chapter Three to spot possible clubhouse problems. In addition, the importance of dealing with reputable and knowledgeable dealers cannot be overemphasized. One should try to deal only with honest people who are more interested in building a long-term business relationship than making a quick buck, and who have the knowledge to steer a collector clear of clubhouse problems. Collectors should also consider the advantages of obtaining appropriate certificates of authenticity from dealers and letters of authenticity from qualified authenticators, a subject addressed in Chapter Five.

Notes

1. The term "forgery" is often used to describe a baseball that is signed in modern times by someone who attempts to reproduce a valuable signature and thereby profit by fraudulently representing and selling the ball as authentic. That use of the term, which is quite common, is not technically correct because the term has a specific legal meaning that refers to the unauthorized execution of a contract or other writing so that such execution purports to be the act of another, or the unauthorized alteration of the writing of another.

2. Sometimes the term "secretarial" is used to describe a clubhouse signature on a baseball. The terms have become interchangeable.

3. Associated Press, February 12, 1996.

4. *Kansas City Star,* February 18, 1996, C13. That figure is probably exaggerated. At the rate of eight dozen per day, assuming a 154-game regular season (at the time), even if team balls were signed in the clubhouse only at home games, that figure implies team ball production at the rate of approximately 7,400 balls per season (with still more being signed during the World Series). There is no evidence for that level of production, even from the Yankees, who probably signed more team balls than any other team during Bauer's playing career. Based on Bauer's and others' accounts, it is probable that there were days when six to eight dozen balls were placed on a table in the clubhouse for signing, but that was not done every day.

5. *Chicago Tribune,* September 17, 1996, 2.

6. *Boston Globe,* January 11, 1998, E13. Marshall added: "If there was a Hall of Fame for forgeries, I'd be in Cooperstown right now."

7. *Boston Globe,* August 7, 1995, 45. An unidentified Yankees batboy has confirmed that DiMaggio had Pete Sheehy sign for him "on rare occasions," estimating those occasions at "one out of five times." Charlie Vascellaro, "Watch Out for Ghost Signers," *Encyclopedia of Sports Memorabilia & Price Guide,* September 1995, 36.

8. *Boston Globe,* August 7, 1995, 45. Former Dodgers pitcher Rex Barney confirmed that, when he was playing (1943, 1946–1950), most ball clubs had personnel who signed for the players. Vascellaro, "Watch Out for Ghost Signers," 34.

9. Bob Brill, "1960s Clubhouse Signer Talks," *The Brill Report,* May 9, 2007 (formerly at http://www.bobbrillreport.com/2007/05/1960s_clubhouse.html).

10. "Team Balls Sometimes a Team Effort," *Sweet Spot,* February/March 1997, 6.

11. *USA Today,* January 25, 1991, 8C. ("As the value of baseball autographs continues to escalate, the baseball commissioner's office is concerned about forgeries. There have been reports some players have clubhouse boys and others learn their signatures and sign bats, pictures and balls.")

12. Jim Bouton, *Ball Four* (rev. ed.) (New York: Macmillan, 1990), 30. A corroborating anecdote can be found in David Halberstam's *October 1964* (New

York: Fawcett, 1995), on page 5: "[Steve] Hamilton liked to come to the park early to get such routine chores as baseball signing out of the way. But no matter how early he came in, Mantle had somehow already signed the requisite number of balls. For a long time Hamilton was impressed by Mantle's diligence, and then it struck him that in fact Mantle was *never* the first to arrive, that Hamilton was always there before Mantle. Since Mantle most assuredly did not do his signing at night after a long game, Hamilton even suspected that Pete Previte, the clubhouse boy, came in every morning and signed Mantle's baseballs for him—although he could find no proof of this."

13. Duke Snider (with Bill Gilbert), *The Duke of Flatbush* (New York: Citadel Press, 2002), 29 (emphasis added).

14. Vascellero, "Watch Out for Ghost Signers," 34. Carl Erskine has also confirmed the practices of Charlie the Brow: "Charlie was also responsible for getting some six dozen baseballs signed daily. If some players missed signing the balls, which the club used for various promotions, Charlie would catch a blast from his boss, 'Big' John Griffin. Charlie was smart. He learned how to substitute a signature if his neck was on the line. Out there somewhere are a few bogus signatures penned by the skillful hand of Charlie 'The Brow.' " Carl Erskine, *Tales From the Dodger Dugout* (Champaign, Ill.: Sports Publishing, 2001), 185–187. The authors suspect that Erskine was not speaking literally regarding the quantity of DiGiovanna's creations; there are many more than "a few." See also Frank Graham, Jr., *A Farewell to Heroes* (Carbondale: Southern Illinois University Press, 2003), 229. ("Many an aging Dodger fan now preserves in his rumpus room a baseball whose stitched cover is densely scribbled all over with the various signatures of Charlie the Brow.")

15. Creamer, "Hey Mister," 106.

16. John M. Mitnick pioneered the identification of Brooklyn Dodgers clubhouse signatures in the early 1990s; see Richard Simon, "Chasing Campy," *Beckett Sports Collectibles Vintage,* March 2002, 54.

17. Ibid. ("When dealing with team-signed baseballs, be aware of a side panel that's 'autographed' by Jackie Robinson, Roy Campanella and Carl Erskine. . . . It could be a signed clubhouse baseball. Collector John Mitnick discovered this a number of years ago.")

18. Creamer, "Hey Mister," 106.

19. *Boston Globe,* August 7, 1995, 45.

20. Associated Press, February 12, 1996.

21. Vascellaro, "Watch Out for Ghost Signers," 34.

22. An unidentified former Major League public relations director has been quoted as follows: "A batboy or a clubhouse person was not considered to be sinful because they were really providing people with happiness. It was never measured in terms of how it affected the marketplace. Those who did sign back then probably feel more guilt today when they see the things they signed for sale." Vascellero, "Watch Out for Ghost Signers," 35.

23. Toward the end of the 1934 season, the *Sporting News* reported the following:

> Many boys, it is said, are finding that there is a ready market for the big names of the game. Signatures scrawled across balls and scorecards are hawked about at prices varying with the reputation of the signers. There are scrambles for fouls knocked into the stands, and the retriever carries the ball for the batter to sign, after which the sphere may be sold to someone who is willing to pay for it as a souvenir. There is a brisk barter for such articles among boys. Youngsters—and even men—have been observed outside of ball parks, offering autographed balls for sale to passersby.

"Mercenary Souvenir-Hunters," *Sporting News,* September 20, 1934, 4. In 1937, Johnny Evers' team ball from the 1924 Tour of Europe (which included members of the New York Giants and the Chicago White Sox) sold for over $1,000, a huge sum at the time, in a charity auction conducted on the air by two Upstate New York radio stations. *Sporting News,* February 18, 1937, 2.

There is a fascinating vignette from 1921 involving Babe Ruth. Before an exhibition game in Louisville, Kentucky, a man approached Ruth and shook his hand. Then the man remarked that he had traveled 100 miles "to shake hands with a man who made $50,000 a year." Ruth's reaction clearly implied that autographed baseballs (or at least those signed by him) already had monetary value and were sold: "'That seemed to be all that guy had in mind,' he said. 'Just thinking about the money I make, or he thinks I make. Reckon if I'd given him an autographed ball he'd peddled it around the pawn shops or put it up at auction to see what he could realize on it. And then they talk about us ball players being money mad!'" *Sporting News,* September 8, 1921, 4.

24. Bill Malone, a clubhouse manager for the Cleveland Indians in the 1960s who signed clubhouse signatures (and later a police officer), made the following interesting statement regarding the practice in a 2007 interview: "I didn't feel strange but I didn't like it and I didn't consider it fraud but I don't know why I didn't." Brill, "1960s Clubhouse Signer Talks." The implication is that the practice was so normal and accepted at the time that virtually no one "on the inside" seriously questioned it, but in hindsight, especially with the values of team balls rising, the practice seems fraudulent.

25. Snider, *The Duke of Flatbush,* 34.

26. The following 2007 anecdote is a case in point: "A few years ago this reporter was asked to sell a baseball owned by the daughter of former Dodger pitcher and minor league manager Chet Kehn. She said Kehn was given the team signed ball by his best friend, Pee Wee Reese after the last game of the 1955 World Series in the clubhouse. As it turned out every signature was a 'clubhouse signature' signed by Charlie DiGiovanna. The ball could have been worth upwards of $15,000 but was relegated to the $200 range." Brill, "1960s Clubhouse Signer Talks."

27. Referring to the recollections of Bill Malone, a clubhouse manager for the Cleveland Indians during the 1960s, from a 2007 interview, Bob Brill wrote: "The fact not all the signatures [were] authentic didn't matter to management at the time he said. In fact, he'd usually get a call from the front office telling him to bring up a few baseballs for a client right away. When he explained not everyone had signed including the starting pitcher the normal answer from the front office, 'sign their name on the ball and bring it up.' So he did as he was ordered because as he says 'It was part of my job.' " Brill, "1960s Clubhouse Signer Talks."

28. As Bill Malone recounted, referring broadly to Major League teams of the time: "If a clubbie signed regularly for a super star they were usually tipped pretty heavy for it, they'd take care of them." Brill, "1960s Clubhouse Signer Talks."

29. An unidentified Los Angeles Dodgers "staffer" was quoted recently as stating: "Having a clubhouse signature would be severely frowned upon. The players are signing themselves, which is the way it should be. To do otherwise would be deceptive." "Team Balls Sometimes a Team Effort," 7–8.

FIVE

CERTIFICATES AND LETTERS OF AUTHENTICITY

A collector's first and best line of defense against forgeries and clubhouse signatures is his or her own knowledge and experience. There is no substitute for developing one's own expertise by using the information provided in this book and in other publications, by viewing as many team balls as possible, and by speaking with knowledgeable dealers and other collectors. Considering the many thousands of different signatures that can be encountered on team balls, however, and the fact that developing real expertise requires a tremendous amount of time and effort, it is often advisable for a collector to gain protection and peace of mind by obtaining a guarantee of authenticity from the seller when purchasing a ball and by seeking the opinion of an expert, especially when purchasing high-priced items.

In recent years, in the face of increasing revelations of non-authentic signatures in the autograph market (see Chapters Three and Four), and the resulting increasing and well-founded nervousness among collectors, many dealers have begun providing a certificate of authenticity (COA) with each autographed item that they sell. A COA can be a separate document or can be incorporated into a receipt or bill of sale. A cottage industry of "authenticators" has also arisen (some of whom call themselves "forensic experts"), who will examine an autographed item and issue a letter of authenticity (LOA) for a fee. The main distinction between a COA and an LOA is that a COA guarantees that the signatures on a certain item are authentic (i.e.,

FUNCTIONS OF AN LOA

An LOA for a team ball has three primary functions: (1) providing comfort for the purchaser; (2) proving authenticity to a third party; and (3) depending on the existence and terms of an applicable COA, possibly determining whether an item may be returned to the seller of the ball for a refund. Figure 5.1 depicts an example of an LOA; this one is for a World Championship 1959 Los Angeles Dodgers team ball.

Comfort for the Purchaser

The first function of an LOA is to give the purchaser comfort that the ball he or she is purchasing is authentic. Authenticity is paramount; it is more important than any other aspect of a team ball, because if a ball is not authentic there is simply no reason for a collector to own it. A non-authentic team ball has no claim to representing a team or being an artifact of baseball history.

The more confidence a collector can have that an item is authentic, the more comfortable he or she will feel regarding the investment and in making the ball a part of a collection. An LOA from a reputable expert goes a long way toward reassuring the buyer that he or she has purchased an authentic item and can represent it to family, friends, and a future purchaser as such.

Proof of Authenticity to a Third Party

The second function of an LOA is proving the authenticity of a team ball to a third party, such as an insurance company for purposes of scheduling the ball on an insurance policy or in case of loss or damage, or to a subsequent purchaser. Its usefulness in that regard depends on the following factors: (1) the expertise of the person signing the LOA; (2) the reputation of the person signing the LOA; and (3) the specificity with which the item is described in the LOA.

Expertise

For third parties, the expertise of the person who signs an LOA is paramount, because dealers and so-called authenticators vary significantly in

Letter of Authenticity

Submission Number: 8405
Date: Monday, February 19, 2007
Subject: 1959 World Champion Los Angeles Dodgers
Field: Baseball
Description: Team-Signed Baseball

Manufacturer: Spalding
Type: Official National League
Executive: Warren C. Giles
Era: 52-69
HOFers: Snider, Reese, Alston, Koufax & Drysdale
Notables: Hodges & Bessent
Quantity of Signatures: 30
Location: All Panels
Writing Implement: Ballpoint Pen
Color: Blue

Certification Number: B38179

This document shall serve of a letter of authenticity for the aforementioned item, which James Spence Authentication, LLC has thoroughly examined.

The signature(s) is/are consistent considering a wide range of specific qualities including slant, flow, pen pressure, letter size and formation, and other characteristics typical of our extensive database of known exemplars we have examined throughout our hobby and professional careers.

It is our considered opinion that the signature item is genuine. Your item has been assigned a unique certification number, which is uploaded into our restricted database and can be confirmed on our website www.SpenceLOA.com at any time. This letter must appear on our proprietary water-marked paper and bear the live signatures of both James Spence and a notary public.

We appreciate your consideration of entrusting James Spence Authentication's judgment and look forward to examining additional collectibles for you in the near future.

Autographically yours,

James J. Spence, Jr.
Managing Member
James Spence Authentication, LLC

COMMONWEALTH OF PENNSYLVANIA
COUNTY OF SCHUYLKILL

Before me, the undersigned notary public, this day personally appeared JAMES J. SPENCE, JR 130 BROOKSHIRE LANE, ORWIGSBURG, PA 17961, to me known who being duly sworn according to law, claimed this to be a true document.

Sworn and subscribed to before me on February 19, 2007.

Notary Public

NOTARIAL SEAL
MARK J MIGLIONICO
Notary Public
EAST BRUNSWICK TWP, SCHUYLKILL COUNTY
My Commission Expires Dec 5, 2009

JSA James Spence Authentication *follow the leader*

130 Brookshire Lane · Orwigsburg, PA 17961-9505 · Toll Free: 888-4JSPENCE · Phone: 570-943-7724 · Fax: 570-943-7719

www.SpenceLOA.com

Figure 5.1. Sample letter of authenticity, issued by James Spence Authentication for a 1959 Los Angeles Dodgers team ball (World Champions).

their knowledge of autographs and other elements of team balls. There are no barriers to calling oneself an authenticator. Indeed there are authenticators who have little or no knowledge of the items that they are authenticating. Some authenticators might be downright dishonest.[5]

Obviously, if one obtains an LOA from someone who does not have sufficient expertise, that LOA is worthless. If, on the other hand, one obtains an LOA from someone with vast and sophisticated knowledge of team balls, that LOA might have great value in establishing authenticity, depending on the degree to which that knowledge is recognized in the marketplace.

Reputation

The reputation of an authenticator can be just as important as, or unfortunately even more important than, his or her level of expertise. It is often said, with respect to many aspects of life, that perception is more important than reality, and the value of an LOA is certainly subject to that principle.

An LOA is of no value in persuading third parties of the authenticity of a team ball unless it is from a recognized and reputable source. One might have an LOA from the most knowledgeable expert on team balls who has ever lived, but if no one else knows of or recognizes that person's expertise, that LOA will not have any persuasive value to a third party. Conversely, one might have an LOA from a widely known sports memorabilia dealer who in fact has little knowledge of team balls (although he or she might have expertise in another area of sports collectibles, such as sports cards), and the mere recognition of that dealer's name might give the LOA credence. It goes without saying that an LOA from a known charlatan has no value; in fact, in the eyes of a third party, it might have a negative effect on perceived authenticity, and presenting it could be worse than not having an LOA at all.

SPECIFICITY

The specificity with which a team ball is described in a COA or an LOA is no less important than the preceding factors, but is often overlooked by dealers, authenticators, and collectors. If it cannot be established conclusively that a COA relates uniquely to a particular team ball, then it might be difficult or impossible for the purchaser to exercise his right of return. If it cannot be established conclusively that an LOA relates uniquely to a particular team ball, then a third party has no basis on which to accord the LOA any weight in determining the authenticity of the ball. For example, if one purchases a 1975 Cincinnati Reds team ball from a reputable dealer, and, as is all too often the case, the dealer provides a COA that merely refers to a "1975 Reds team ball" without more identifying information, how can it be proved that the COA relates to that particular ball? After all, there are probably hundreds of 1975 Reds team balls in existence.

A few of the major dealers in modern single-signature and theme balls (balls signed by players who fit a certain theme, such as 500 home run hitter balls) have recognized that problem. They perceived that their preprinted COAs were not attached to the balls with which they were issued and could not be made more specific (because there is usually not any unique feature of a modern mass-produced single-signature ball that could be expressed in writing), and therefore that they were virtually useless for proving authenticity.

As a solution, they started to implement special markings, such as holograms and decals, which are permanently attached to the signed ball as a mark of authenticity. The marking is designed to serve as proof that the ball was signed under the supervision of the dealer and is therefore authentic, relying for its effectiveness on the reputation of the dealer. Sometimes the hologram or decal contains a unique serial number that is linked to a separate COA that also contains that serial number.

A similar marking system should not be used for team balls for a variety of reasons, not the least of which is that the entire ball is usually used for signatures, and a hologram would detract from the appearance of the ball. The uniqueness of individual team balls, however, facilitates the effective use of COAs and LOAs. Many variables can and should be mentioned in a COA or LOA that are useful in proving that the document was issued for a specific ball. For example, the COA or LOA should state the following characteristics of the ball:

1. The exact number of signatures on the ball, including whether any player signed more than once;
2. The color(s) of ink used to sign the ball;

3. Information regarding the baseball, including (a) the manufacturer and whether it is an Official American or National League, World Series, or All-Star ball (and, if not, the model or other information stamped on the ball), (b) the color of the stitching (some older balls and modern All-Star Game balls were made with two alternating colors of stitching), and (c) if the ball is Official, the league president's signature printed on the ball; and
4. Any other significant identifying marks or characteristics, such as a date or a coating.

More specificity can and should be added when possible by actually listing all of the signatures on the ball, and even listing them according to their positions on the ball, which can be accomplished by referring to the sweet spot of the ball and each panel's position in relation to the sweet spot using directional terms (north, south, east, and west), or by starting at the top of one panel and moving down that panel, across the sweet spot, and up the next panel, and then doing the same for the other two panels. Considering the astronomical odds against two team balls being exactly alike in terms of signature placement, the addition of specificity to a COA or LOA can make it very clear to a third party that it relates to a specific ball. Specificity in a COA or LOA is critical, because unless that relation can be established with certainty, the document is worthless to a third party.

Recently, aided by advances in digital photography and printer technology, some dealers, auctions, and authenticators have initiated the practice of including actual color photographs of items in their COAs or LOAs. Since every autographed item is unique, inclusion of a photograph on a COA or LOA is a highly effective method of linking the document to the item. As time goes on, it is hoped that inclusion of photographs in all COAs and LOAs will become standard.

Unfortunately, at least for a brief time, several "authenticators" adopted the practice of writing a serial number and initialing on items that they "authenticated." Such practices deface the item and thus detract from its appearance and value. When submitting a team ball for authentication, the owner of the item should always inquire about the authentication process and insist that no visible markings be placed on the ball itself.

PROVENANCE

In addition to being helpful in establishing a guarantee, a COA can also serve as a letter of provenance that establishes the origin of the ball. Aside from its significance for a collector, establishing provenance might tangibly increase the value of a team ball if, for example, the ball was originally owned by a famous player or other baseball personality. That is especially true when that former owner is associated with the team that signed the ball or a famous event that occurred during the season in which the ball was signed. For example, in 1997 a rather ordinary 1961 Yankees team ball was sold at auction for over $12,000, which was then several times the prevailing market value of such a ball (if completely authentic). The reason was that the ball had belonged to Mickey Mantle.

Whenever a collector obtains any team ball from a significant source like a player, or from any source who knows an interesting story about the origin of the ball, the COA should also include the provenance of the ball. Too many of those wonderful stories or associations have been lost over the years because such information was not obtained in writing, or, once obtained, was lost. In a very real sense, team ball collectors are the custodians of part of the history of our national game, and therefore we have a responsibility to future generations to preserve that history. A COA that includes provenance can be a significant means of such preservation, especially if it is issued by a reputable source.

As a word of caution, a collector should always remember that the concepts of authenticity and provenance are separate and distinct, and that provenance is never a substitute for authenticity (see Chapter Three). Just because a player or other famous person owned a team ball does not mean that the signatures are authentic. For example, the authors have seen many team balls owned by players that had clubhouse signatures. Authenticity must always be separately established.

CONCLUSION

COAs have become common in the hobby and can be a significant means of protection for collectors, but often they are not worded correctly. By relying on the advice in this chapter, a collector can ensure that he or she receives a meaningful COA in connection with each purchase, at least in the sense that it serves the guarantee function of a COA. A COA says nothing about actual authenticity unless it comes from a truly knowledgeable and reputable source.

While LOAs do not guarantee authenticity (it would be unreasonable to expect what amounts to an insurance policy for a relatively small authentication fee), they are useful in providing the considered opinion of an expert. It has become common for purchasers to obtain LOAs, especially for team balls of significant value, and many sellers and auction firms obtain and offer them with team balls as a standard practice. The reason is that LOAs often provide significant comfort that the ball is authentic and thus confer value on the ball in the marketplace.

Notes

1. In drawing the distinction between COAs and LOAs, the authors are recognizing the practice that has arisen in the sports memorabilia industry while at the same time defining and prescribing terminology in a manner that we believe will be helpful. It is, of course, possible for a seller of an autographed item to be a recognized expert and therefore have the ability to issue an LOA that would confer value on the item in the marketplace. Some professional authentication firms have chosen to require their employees to refrain from dealing in autographs in order to avoid actual or apparent conflicts of interest.

2. When dealing with a team ball, ideally the COA should state that the guarantee of authenticity applies to all signatures on the ball except any that are specified to be non-authentic (for example, clubhouse). That properly puts the onus on the seller to disclose which signatures are questionable and therefore not subject to the guarantee.

3. We use the term "dealer" to refer to one who offers an item for sale at a certain price, in contrast to an auction company, which holds auctions in which items are sold to the highest bidder. As common as it is for dealers to accept a return for any reason within a short period of time after a sale, it is equally uncommon for an auction house to do so. As explained later in this chapter, guarantees offered by auctions usually allow returns only during a limited period of time after the conclusion of the auction and only in cases in which an item turns out not to be authentic.

4. When an item is purchased from an auction house, sometimes a COA is not issued, but rather the guarantee of authenticity is stated in the terms and conditions of sale at the beginning of the auction catalog. The collector should review those terms and conditions carefully before bidding, noting particularly the terms of the guarantee of authenticity, and then keep a copy on file with a copy of the purchase receipt.

5. It is always wise to remember a warning included by the FBI on its Operation Bullpen website: "Certificates of authenticity are not guarantees of authenticity. Individuals and companies involved with selling forged memorabilia often include a Certificate of Authenticity, allegedly from a third party expert. Often, the authenticator is either a knowing or unknowing, but incompetent, participant in the fraud." (Note: In that statement the FBI uses the term "certificate of authenticity" to refer to what we define as an LOA.)

SIX

GRADING

The grading of a team ball is the process of rating its physical condition according to a scale that has a well-defined and generally accepted meaning to collectors and dealers. Grading is entirely distinct from the process of authentication, but condition—which grading aims to describe—can be almost as important as authenticity in determining the monetary value of a ball.

As in the case of all antiques and collectibles, the condition of a team ball has a profound effect on its value (see Chapter Seven), and it is not unusual for a ball in superlative condition to command a price several times higher than an otherwise identical ball in lesser condition. It is also axiomatic that the better the condition of a team ball, the more likely it will hold its value or appreciate in value over time. That axiom is true because collectors generally seek balls in the best condition available; therefore, the better the condition, the higher the demand (and likely the lower the supply), and, as a result, the higher the value.

Two grading scales are presently in common use. The more prevalent is a verbally descriptive scale that ranges from "Mint" at the high end down to "Poor" at the bottom end, with the following five intermediate grades (from highest to lowest): "Near-Mint," "Excellent," "Very Good," "Good," and "Fair." That scale is referred to in this chapter as the Verbal Scale. The other scale, which is referred to in this chapter as the Numerical Scale, grades team balls from 1 to 10 (10 being the highest and 1 the lowest). Both scales were originally borrowed from the realm of sports cards and adapted to team balls (the Verbal Scale was probably originally borrowed from coin grading and adapted to sports cards). Sometimes, a grader will give a team ball two separate grades, one relating to the condition of the ball itself and the other to the condition of the signatures, or one combined grade, using both the Verbal Scale and the Numerical Scale, in which the two ratings correspond to each other (e.g., "Mint 10").

Despite the use of the two scales, the grading of a team ball is and will remain a subjective exercise, for two principal reasons. First, the scales themselves are vague, and the gradations within them do not have any universally accepted meaning. Second, even if collectors and dealers were, hypothetically, to convene a meeting, choose a scale, and promulgate specific, universally accepted definitions for the various grades within it, the process of grading would still remain highly subjective. There are just too many subjective condition factors to consider—the toning of the baseball, the strength of the signatures, the strength of the stamping, the existence and condition of a coating, and so forth—each of which, in turn, has its own range of nuances. Those many factors combine to produce the overall aesthetic appearance of a ball, which is really what most collectors are ultimately interested in knowing when they are deciding whether to make a purchase and how much to pay. Unfortunately, that overall aesthetic appearance is very difficult to describe using a set of shorthand grades.

Before the advent of the Internet and the mass adoption of digital photography, grading scales were very important and necessary for purposes of efficiency. Ideally, every collector would want to examine a team ball in person before making a purchase decision, but that is usually not feasible, except in limited circumstances such as sports memorabilia shows or local shops. Fortunately, the Internet and e-mail are now making it possible to transmit photographs cheaply and instantaneously, with the result that today most balls are purchased after the buyer has seen detailed color photographs.

Relatively recently, however, grading has taken on a new dimension and importance. Several professional authenticators have begun grading team balls, marketing their service as potentially enhancing their value. Just as the grading scales themselves were borrowed from the realm of sports cards and applied to autographed baseballs, so has the practice of encapsulating and grading sports cards (which has been very successful) now been applied to autographed baseballs, including team balls. The question is whether the grading of an autographed baseball adds value to it.

Certainly the authentication of an autographed baseball by a recognized expert confers value on that ball. The reason is that authenticity is not easily recognized; it requires significant expertise, obtained over a long period of time, to be able to authenticate any autographed baseball. The greatest level of expertise is required to authenticate a team ball, because a large number of different signatures must be authenticated. With all of the authenticity issues that apply to team balls, including forgeries, clubhouse signatures, rubber stamps, and tracing (see Chapters Three and Four), the ability to authenticate a team ball is very rare; even if one possesses it, unless that ability is generally recognized in the marketplace, it does not confer any value on a ball. Since a collector is willing to pay for a team ball only because it is, in fact, authentic, an expert opinion that proves such authenticity to the satisfaction of the collector and subsequent potential purchasers has significant value. In a very real sense such an opinion protects the collector's investment in the ball.

The value conferred by professional grading of an autographed baseball is, however, more dubious. Unlike authenticity, condition is purely aesthetic—what matters is whether, and the extent to which, the appearance of the ball is pleasing to the viewer. One need not be an expert to make that determination. If one were to show a 1955 Dodgers team ball totally filled with clubhouse signatures, but in mint condition, to someone without any authentication expertise, and ask him to describe the condition, undoubtedly he would use any number of superlatives. If one were then to ask that person if the signatures are authentic, assuming he is honest he would have to respond by saying that he has no idea.

Another problem with the grading of autographed baseballs is the range of factors that affect their condition. Some might argue, not without merit, that subtle color variations and the appearance of tiny print dots and the like, as well as the practice of shaving the edges of a card in order to remove imperfections, make grading the condition of sports cards as complex as grading team balls. Still, it seems obvious that the number of significant variables applicable to team balls, and the range of each of those variables, far exceed those applicable to sports cards. Except for objectively measurable factors such as differences in centering, all sports cards were originally mass produced and theoretically started out essentially identical, whereas each team ball is unique in many respects from the moment that it is originally signed. No two team balls can ever be exactly alike.

Those who advocate or sell grading services for autographed baseballs might argue that it is not the grading of the ball per se that adds value, but rather (1) the rating of the ball by an expert according to a recognized scale, and (2) the development of "population" records (as has been done with cards) to indicate the relative rarity of high-grade examples of different balls. It seems, however, that the value of the rating might be negligible, for two reasons. First, as discussed earlier, anyone should be able to determine the level of aesthetic attractiveness of a ball simply by viewing it. Just because a so-called "expert" certifies that a ball is "Near-Mint 8.5" does not make the ball look any better or worse. Second, the scale used for the grade might not be sufficiently well defined for the assigned grade to convey generally understood meaning to the marketplace, and even if it were well defined, the grading of a ball remains a subjective exercise.

The development of population records is a potentially different matter. If a professional grading service were to develop a critical mass of grading records for a certain category of ball (e.g., 1961 Yankees team balls), then those data, combined with the grade assigned to a particular ball, might offer perspective on the relative rarity of a ball in that condition, which could add value to the ball. The problem is that no one knows how many 1961 Yankees team balls exist, and no one will ever know that with any certainty. Therefore, if a collector pays a large sum for the only "Mint 9" 1961 Yankees ball on record—assuming that it is the only one—another "Mint 9" example, or even five or ten more (for example, in the collection of a team member or official), could suddenly surface. The probability of multiple examples of that quality suddenly surfacing might be low, but the possibility certainly exists.

It can be argued that the same problems afflict sports card grading, and yet it seems clear that grading has enhanced the value of such cards. Indeed, a separate market for graded sports cards has developed, with some commanding tremendous prices. It remains to be seen whether the grading of autographed baseballs follows a similar path. Ultimately the market will decide. In Chapter Seven we analyze the market for team balls and how values are determined.

SEVEN

VALUATION

Let us say that you have found a team ball that you want to add to your collection. Perhaps it is being sold in an auction, or perhaps a dealer is offering it for sale outright for a specific price. How do you know how much you should pay for it? How do you know what it is worth? On rare occasions, a particular collector might have the financial resources and the desire to pay just about any price for a ball that he or she has an overwhelming desire to own, and in that instance the question of valuation is practically irrelevant. The rest of the time, however, and for the rest of us, understanding the principles of valuation is very important in guiding our purchase (and sale) decisions.

This book does not contain a team ball price guide. Although the creation of such a guide has been attempted, it is doubtful that a useful price guide can be produced for team balls because of the uniqueness of each ball and the dynamic nature of the market. It is of little informative value to say, for example, that a 1969 Mets team ball is worth $2,000 simply because a 1969 Mets team ball might have sold recently for that price. The reason is that 1969 Mets team balls routinely sell for much more and much less than that figure, depending on numerous factors, and even that same hypothetical ball that sold for $2,000 could sell for a substantially different price if it were sold again six months or a year later—or even the next day.

That is not to say that information about past sales is useless in determining the value of a ball. Indeed, such information can be extremely useful as an indication of the range of value, especially if the sales were recent and accurate descriptive information is available regarding the balls that

in determining team championships for that season (and also, for that matter, individual player awards). Playoffs and a World Series are held annually at the end of each regular season based solely on the results of play during that season. Team rosters have effect only within a specific season, and the rules that govern roster changes apply only within that season. When the next season begins the following year, each franchise's win-loss slate is wiped clean, each one starts over again with a new roster, and all players start fresh with new individual season statistics. Nothing is inherited from past seasons, and nothing will carry forward to future seasons. In other words, team name and year are the "units of measure" that classify and identify a team, and therefore, by extension, a team ball. There is a real qualitative difference between team balls from different teams and different years; each team ball represents a unique team and unique events that, by definition, cannot be represented by a team ball from a different team and year.

Thus, a collector chooses to purchase a team ball precisely because it represents a particular team and year that hold significance for him or her. Very rarely, if ever, does a collector decide that he or she would like to own just any team ball from a particular team (regardless of the year) or any team ball from a particular year (regardless of the team). Instead, the collector decides that he or she would like to own, for example, a 1966 Braves team ball (the franchise's first season in Atlanta) or a 1995 Braves team ball (the team's first, and so far only, World Championship since moving to Atlanta). No ball from another team or another year can serve as a substitute, because it is a fundamentally different "product." A 1994 Braves team ball simply cannot substitute for a 1995 Braves team ball, nor can a 1995 Dodgers team ball do so; they are fundamentally different goods, lacking the characteristics of the 1995 Braves ball that are important to the collector (i.e., the fact that it represents a unique team with a specific roster and record of performance).

It is, of course, very common for a collector to have an overall theme (or sometimes multiple themes) for his or her collection. For example, some collectors have a favorite team and seek to collect a "run" of team balls from that team. A run, in this context, refers to a set of team balls from a period of a team's existence consisting of one team ball from each year. As another example, some collectors seek to collect a run of championship team balls, which might include the World Champion team and possibly its World Series opponent (the other league champion team) from each year. Still other collectors might seek to accumulate a set of team balls from a year that is particularly significant or memorable for the collector. Even in all of those cases, however, the collector is making decisions to purchase individual team balls from specific teams and years in order to complete the overall collection. A ball from a specific team and year is required to fill each slot in the desired collection, and no other team ball will fill that slot.

Occasionally, a collector will desire to own examples of team balls from certain famous eras of specific teams. As an illustration, a collector might want to own an example of a team ball from the St. Louis Cardinals' "Gas House Gang" of the 1930s, or perhaps a team ball from the Yankees' record five consecutive World Championships (1949–1953). In those limited instances, to a particular buyer, team balls from different years might substitute for each other. Even those collectors often have preferences for certain years over others, however, and in any case the vast majority of buyers who would be interested in purchasing a particular team ball are seeking a team ball from a specific team and year.

Therefore, there is a separate market for team balls from a specific team and year, because that is how collectors generally define the product in making purchasing decisions, and because team balls from other teams and other years generally cannot be substitutes for them. Not surprisingly, team balls are always described and advertised for sale in that manner.

The Buyers and Sellers

Now that we have defined the extent of the market, we can also identify the buyers and sellers in the market. The buyers are simply those collectors who seek to purchase a team ball from a specific team and year (e.g., a 1948 Indians team ball). The sellers are simply those dealers, collectors, former players, or others who possess an example of that team ball and are willing to sell it.

Identifying those two groups completes our definition of the market for team balls and also leads directly to our next topic: supply and demand. Our identification of the sellers begs the central question of supply: how many examples of each team ball are available, and which team balls are the most common and the rarest? Likewise, our identification of the buyers begs the central question of demand: why do the buyers seek to purchase team balls, and which balls are in the greatest demand?

SUPPLY AND DEMAND

The basic model of supply and demand has been called "the workhorse of microeconomics."[3] It tells us how price (and therefore value) is determined for a product. Although team balls are not the fungible commodities or products to which the supply and demand model is most appropriately applied, the basic principles of supply and demand are certainly applicable to team balls and other collectibles. Generally speaking, assuming static supply, higher demand leads to higher prices, and lower demand leads to lower prices. Assuming static demand, less abundant supply leads to higher prices, and more abundant supply leads to lower prices. There is even some elasticity in the supply and demand curves as applied to team balls, as with other more conventional products. For example, as the price of a certain ball (e.g., a 1932 Yankees team ball) rises, the supply of 1932 Yankees balls on the market can be expected to increase somewhat, as more owners of such a ball will be induced to sell. Similarly, if the price of a 1932 Yankees team ball drops, the demand for that ball can be expected to increase, as more collectors can afford to purchase one and will seek to do so.

Supply

Turning first to supply, we have defined the product as team balls from a particular team and year. Therefore, the supply is the number of such balls that are offered for sale in the market over a given period of time. That number is random, varying from time to time based on the independent and unpredictable actions of numerous sellers, and it represents a small portion of the number of such balls that exist (a number that can never be known with any degree of certainty because it is not possible to produce an inventory of all team balls in existence). The best we can do is to form an opinion on the relative rarity of different balls based on anecdotal evidence of the number of balls that reach the open market over a certain period of time.

The team ball is fundamentally unlike the mass-produced, manufactured "collectibles" that flood the sports memorabilia market today. Team balls have always been and remain naturally scarce, because by their nature they can be created only during a particular season and in limited quantities. The only exceptions are reunion balls or team balls created by a collector or dealer spending the time and money to obtain signatures over time by mail or at autograph shows or other events. Of course, those exceptions are also limited in quantity, depend on team members remaining healthy and cooperating, and lack the originality (and therefore often the full value) of an original season team ball.

Obviously some team balls are rarer than others. One of the main reasons for rarity is age; the further we look back in time, the fewer balls were signed, and the more likely it is that a significant percentage of the balls that were signed have been lost, destroyed, or damaged or degraded to the point of losing their appeal to a collector. Major League teams have included the signing of team balls (particularly in championship years) in their regular routines since the 1920s or 1930s, with isolated examples of team balls existing from as far back as approximately 1910, but the number of balls signed in a season started out very small and has gradually increased over time (see Chapter Two). Today all Major League teams sign team balls practically every day of the season, whether they are at home or on the road.

Based on anecdotal evidence of the balls that have come to the open market in recent years, all team balls from years before 1940 are relatively scarce. Many collectors do not realize just how scarce many of those balls are, and many such balls, even those from less famous or successful teams, contain rare Hall of Fame and star players' and coaches' signatures.

Most championship and All-Star team balls from any year prior to 1950 are also rare, although there are notable exceptions. For example, Yankees team balls are often not particularly uncommon, but they are nonetheless expensive because of high demand. To say that pre-1950 championship team balls are generally rare, however, is not to say that all post-1950 team balls are plentiful. How many collectors own a complete 1950 Phillies ("Whiz Kids") ball, or a 1961 Reds ball, or even a 1981 Dodgers ball? Not many.

We do not know the exact reason why some of the modern years are scarce. The main reason is probably that certain clubs in certain years did not sign very many balls, as a result of either low demand, cost-consciousness, or lack of motivation on the part of players or clubhouse staff. Another reason could be lack of wide distribution in certain years; it is possible that certain clubs distributed balls only to players and coaches, and that those persons or their families are still holding quantities of team balls. In time, many of those balls will probably find their way into the marketplace, but balls from those years probably will continue to be relatively scarce. A third reason could be that collectors and fans have already absorbed the vast majority of available balls and are unwilling to part with them, although that should apply only in situations of extremely high and long-standing demand, as in the case of 1955 Brooklyn Dodgers team balls (a popular team and the year of their only World Championship).

Supply is a very important factor influencing the value of a team ball. That is why a savvy collector might pay as much for a 1961 Reds team ball—a National League championship team with a relatively undistinguished roster (except for Frank Robinson)—as for a 1955 Yankees American League championship ball including some of the all-time greats, such as Yogi Berra, Whitey Ford, Mickey Mantle, and Phil Rizzuto. The 1961 Reds ball is much rarer.

As noted previously, one can determine the relative scarcity of championship and All-Star team balls only from anecdotal evidence supplied by the market over time. Figure 7.1 is a list of post-1940 championship team balls that the authors believe are particularly scarce, especially relative to demand. The list is based on anecdotal evidence of the supply of original season, substantially complete, and totally authentic team balls from a particular year. The balls on the list are not necessarily more valuable than balls that are not on the list; they are merely less plentiful.

Demand

Demand for team balls results from an emotional attraction to the game of baseball itself, the history of the game, or a particular player or team. As a result, the demand is highest where the emotional attraction is the strongest and the most widespread. The primary determinants of demand are the team's performance, roster, and location. Those are the factors that a collector will contemplate first in determining whether he or she wants to purchase a team ball for his or her collection. Those factors, and their effect on demand, can readily be understood by classifying team balls as either "General Demand" or "Specific Demand."

1941 Brooklyn Dodgers

1942 St. Louis Cardinals

1945 Detroit Tigers and Chicago Cubs

1946 Boston Red Sox

1947 Brooklyn Dodgers

1948 Cleveland Indians

1950 Philadelphia Phillies

1951 New York Yankees* and New York Giants*

1952 Brooklyn Dodgers*

1953 Brooklyn Dodgers*

1954 New York Giants*

1955 Brooklyn Dodgers*

1956 Brooklyn Dodgers*

1957 New York Yankees*

1958 New York Yankees*

1961 New York Yankees* and Cincinnati Reds

1962 New York Yankees* and San Francisco Giants

1963 New York Yankees*

1964 New York Yankees*

1966 Baltimore Orioles

1967 Boston Red Sox

1970 Cincinnati Reds

1971 Pittsburgh Pirates and Baltimore Orioles

1974 Oakland A's and Los Angeles Dodgers

1975 Boston Red Sox

1976 New York Yankees

1977 New York Yankees*

1978 New York Yankees*

1979 Baltimore Orioles

1981 Los Angeles Dodgers

2000 New York Mets

2001 Arizona Diamondbacks

2002 Anaheim Angels

2004 St. Louis Cardinals

2005 Houston Astros

2006 St. Louis Cardinals

2008 Philadelphia Phillies

Figure 7.1. List of scarce (relative to demand) post-1940 championship team balls. An asterisk indicates those that are scarce only in a fully authentic state because of the prevalence of clubhouse or rubber-stamped signatures.

General Demand Team Balls

General Demand team balls are those whose appeal is not tied to sentimental attachment to a specific city or player, but rather to (1) an event (such as the World Series or All-Star Game), or (2) the status of included players (such as a multitude of Hall of Fame or star players), or (3) the sheer age of the ball and its nostalgic value or significance in the history of the game. General Demand team balls are sought by collectors from all over the United States and from a growing number of other countries such as Canada and Japan.

Championship team balls (generally defined as balls signed by the league pennant-winning teams that participated in the World Series, but arguably also including division champions) represent teams with dominant records and also evoke the high drama of the postseason, which inherently appeals to all baseball collectors without regard to the cities represented by the teams or the identities of the players. Team balls of World Championship teams are also naturally sought by more collectors than team balls of League Championship teams (i.e., those teams that were defeated in the World Series), simply because World Championship team balls represent the pinnacle of achievement. All-Star Game team balls appeal to collectors precisely because they represent the "best of the best" from a specific season. Likewise, a team ball with an all-star lineup, such as the Cleveland Indians teams of the mid-1950s, appeals to a wide range of collectors whether they have a sentimental attachment to Cleveland or not. Those who are motivated by nostalgia or are interested in the history of the game often seek older team balls, regardless of whether they represent championship teams.

Specific Demand Team Balls

Specific Demand team balls may be defined as team balls whose appeal to a collector results from the fact that they represent a team from a certain city or that they include a certain player. The primary sources of demand for such balls are collectors of items associated with that specific team or player, although there are other relatively minor sources of demand, such as collectors who are attempting to build a complete set of Major League team balls from a certain year. Demand for Specific Demand team balls is often highly geographic in nature; it is likely to be strongest in the city or region where the team is or was located.

Significance for Value

There is overlap between the two categories. All team balls are Specific Demand team balls. All General Demand team balls are, therefore, also Specific Demand balls, but only a small fraction of Specific Demand team balls also fall into the General Demand category. The relationship between the two categories is best illustrated by the diagram shown in Figure 7.2.

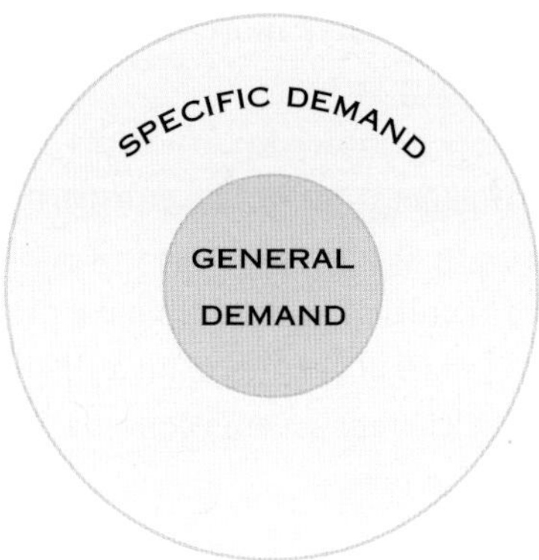

Figure 7.2. Relationship between General Demand and Specific Demand team balls.

The demand is highest where the two categories overlap (in the General Demand circle), simply because the balls that fall into both categories simultaneously have the most collectors desiring to purchase them. Therefore, General Demand balls are in much higher demand relative to Specific Demand balls and generally have higher value (assuming, of course, that supply is not materially different).

Other Factors Affecting Demand

Macroeconomic Conditions. An important influence on the value of team balls that should not be overlooked is the effect of general economic conditions. Collectibles such as team balls do not have any intrinsic value. They do not fulfill any basic human needs. They perform no utilitarian function, they have no nutritional value, and they do not produce oxygen for breathing. They do not pay interest or dividends that can be used to purchase other things, as stocks and bonds do, and they do not function as money, as gold and silver do. In short, team balls are not necessities; purchasing a team ball is a discretionary expenditure. They are properly characterized as hobby or luxury items. They have value only because collectors desire to own them, and they are worth only what someone is willing to pay for them. Therefore the value of team balls is significantly affected by what we have come to know as the "wealth effect." In times of economic prosperity, when salaries and the value of portfolios rise, people feel wealthier, and are therefore willing and able to spend more money on goods and services. They also have more money for discretionary spending on collectibles and luxury items.

Thus, just as the prices of other luxury items such as art and jewelry tend to rise in times of general economic prosperity, so do the prices of team balls. The reverse can also be true; the prices of team balls can drop in times of economic difficulty. The authors have observed, however, that there is always a strong market for the team balls that are in the highest demand. Even during the current severe economic downturn, choice balls have tended to bring strong prices.

The State of the Game and Players' Reputations. It seems counterintuitive that the present popularity of professional baseball might have an impact on the value of team balls from past seasons, especially those from the distant past. After all, balls from past years represent history, which is fixed and cannot be changed. Intuition tells us that, since the past is immutable, what happens today should not affect it. It would seem that since a team ball is a representative artifact of the past, its value should not be affected by today's events.

The problem with our intuition is that the historic significance of a ball (which indeed cannot be changed) is only one factor in determining its value. Value is dependent on what someone is willing to pay for the ball today, and the basis of the value of a team ball is nostalgia and a sentimental attraction to the game and its history. That sense of nostalgia and sentiment can be affected, both positively and negatively, by the present popularity of the game of baseball. By extension, the value of team balls can be affected in the same manner.

That phenomenon occurred during the Major League Baseball strike of 1994–1995. It was clear at that time that the market for baseball memorabilia, including team balls, was depressed. The market roared back after the strike ended and baseball was restored to its prominent place in our culture. Even so, collectors should be generally aware that the value of even their vintage team balls can be affected (positively or negatively) by the popularity of the game of baseball today.

One should also understand how changes in a player's reputation, even years after a team ball was signed, can affect the value of the ball—and such impact is almost never positive. An obvious example is a situation in which a player's use of steroids is revealed years after the fact. If that player's signature is a key signature on a particular team ball, such a revelation can adversely affect the value of that ball.

SIGNIFICANT FACTORS FOR VALUATION

Once a collector has made the decision to purchase a particular team ball (from a specific team and year), the next step is to find a desirable example. Although the methods for acquiring team balls are numerous (see Chapter Eight), it is probable that the collector will not be able to find an example immediately, depending on the rarity of the ball. He or she will have to follow auctions and sale advertisements for a time until an acceptable example comes up for sale.

It was noted at the beginning of this chapter that different examples of the same team ball often sell for widely divergent prices. Four principal factors account for those divergences: condition; completeness; type of baseball; and authenticity. The factors discussed in the section on demand explain why a collector will decide to purchase a ball from a certain team and year. Once that decision has been made, a collector will typically consider those four factors in determining (1) prima facie, whether a certain example is desirable or up to his or her standards, and (2) if so, how much he or she is willing to pay for it. In a sense, those factors may be characterized as secondary factors of demand; for example, we can say that the demand is higher for team balls in superior condition than it is for balls in average or below-average condition, or that the demand is higher for team balls that are more complete. A discussion of each of those factors and its effect on value follows.

Condition

Condition is a crucial determinant of value for any collectible. All tangible objects have the tendency to degrade or be damaged over time, and team balls are particularly subject to damage from many natural and man-made forces. Of course there are very effective techniques for protecting and preserving team balls (see Chapter Nine).

Team ball collectors naturally strive to obtain balls in the best possible condition, taking into account their own budgets and the availability of balls. Indeed, some collectors will purchase only team balls in superlative condition. As time passes, however, the number of pristine examples of any team ball inevitably diminishes, while at the same time the number of collectors has been increasing for several decades. Thus, the competition to obtain examples in the best condition increases (the demand increases relative to supply), and, in accordance with the principles of supply and demand, prices also increase. At the same time, those examples in lesser condition are relatively more plentiful, while the demand for them is not as great, and thus their value is often significantly lower than that of their high-grade counterparts. The value of the lower-grade examples still might increase over time, but at a slower rate than that of the balls in better condition.

The impact on value of even small differences in condition can be dramatic. It is not uncommon for high-grade examples of older championship and All-Star team balls to sell for several times the price of lower-grade examples that are otherwise very similar. Indeed, there are some wealthy collectors who seem to be willing to pay virtually any price for examples of particularly rare and desirable balls in pristine condition.

Completeness

Completeness can be as important as condition in determining the value of a team ball. The very essence of a team ball—what makes it desirable to a collector—is that it contains the signatures of a group of individuals who represent a particular baseball team from a particular season. If one or more of those individuals' signatures are missing (particularly the key signatures; see Chapter One), the ball's value as a true team ball can be reduced.

As in the case of condition, the valuation difference attributable to completeness can be dramatic, with "complete" examples selling for significantly higher prices than incomplete examples. It all depends on the rarity of the ball and the identity of the missing signatures; as one would expect, the absence of a less important key signature has a much less pronounced effect on value than the absence of a more important signature. For example, the absence of Herb Pennock on a 1927 Yankees team ball might cause only a 5–10% discount in value compared to a complete example, while the absence of Babe Ruth on the same ball might cause a discount of 75% or more.

It is often possible to add a missing key signature to a team ball by attending or sending a ball to one of the many autograph shows or private signing sessions held each year. The topic of adding signatures is covered in detail at the end of this chapter.

Type of Baseball

Since the dawn of team balls, all kinds of baseballs have been used for signing. For present purposes, baseballs fall into two general categories: official baseballs and unofficial baseballs.

Official baseballs are manufactured especially for use in Major League games and carry markings to that effect. For that reason, they are manufactured according to strict specifications and quality standards. Unofficial baseballs are not subject to those standards and specifications, and therefore they vary greatly in the quality of materials and workmanship.

Collectors very clearly prefer team balls signed on the appropriate and contemporaneous Official Major League baseball. For example, in deciding between a 1933 New York Giants team ball signed on an Official National League baseball (with the facsimile signature of John Heydler, the president of the National League at that time) and one signed on an unofficial ball of similar condition and completeness, an astute collector will always prefer the official ball and will be willing to pay more for it. It may be said that team balls signed on official balls command a premium price, or perhaps that team balls signed on unofficial balls are discounted somewhat in value. Either way, there is a clear differential in value.

Authenticity

The factor of authenticity has been left to last, but it is certainly not least. It is self-evident that a team ball is of interest to collectors only if it is authentic. If a team ball is not authentic, that is, if all of the signatures are modern forgeries or clubhouse signatures, then the ball has no significance for a collector and the collector has no reason for possessing it. Thus there is no demand for a non-authentic team ball, except as a curiosity or if the baseball itself (apart from the writing on it) is a collectible. Without demand, the ball is worthless.

There are, however, many team balls that are partially authentic and partially non-authentic. Those are primarily team balls with some (but not all) clubhouse signatures. In that case, the presence of non-authentic signatures might reduce but not completely eliminate the demand for the ball (largely depending on how many clubhouse signatures there are and which signatures they are), and therefore the ball still might have value.

ARE TEAM BALLS A GOOD INVESTMENT?

It is not the purpose of this book to give investment advice, or to recommend purchasing team balls as an investment. One should collect team balls primarily because of their historic and sentimental values, and not as a means to make money.

That said, many collectors—and particularly those who have taken the time to acquire the knowledge necessary to make intelligent purchases—have seen the value of their collections grow over time, in some cases dramatically. In an economic sense, in the past, purchasing a team ball has amounted to converting cash into a tangible asset that does not depreciate (unless it is damaged) and that tends to appreciate in value over time. The authors are not aware of any reason why that would change in the future.

CONCLUSION

Although we know the factors that determine value, there is no mathematical formula for making a precise determination for a specific ball. Prices realized in past auctions and dealer ads are useful in determining a rough range of value for a ball, but their usefulness is limited because of the uniqueness of each ball and the dynamic nature of the market. As in the case of other collectibles, the prices of team balls ebb and flow, but the "real" prices (factoring in the effect of monetary inflation) generally move higher over time, especially in the case of higher-quality and more desirable examples. The best way to value team balls is to follow the market closely and develop an intuitive sense of valuation and the direction of the market, assisted by the principles discussed in this chapter.

As more collectors have entered the market, demand for all team balls has naturally risen, and so have prices. Among the best sources for historical price information for team balls are the prices-realized lists and databases on the websites of sports auction firms. The current record price for a team ball in a public auction is $93,666, the price paid in 2000 for the 1919 Chicago White Sox team ball illustrated in Figure 2.4. That record can be expected to be broken in the future.

Now that we have addressed the valuation of team balls, in Chapter Eight we discuss how and where to purchase them. We conclude this chapter with a note on the topic of adding signatures to a team ball.

A NOTE ON ADDING SIGNATURES

A controversial but little-discussed topic is the practice of adding signatures to team balls. The subject is arguably as relevant to preservation as it is to the subject of this chapter. It seems, however, that the primary motivation in adding a signature to a team ball is to enhance the completeness and therefore the value of the ball, and that is why signature additions are covered here.

One frequently encounters a team ball that is missing one or more key signatures. Often those individuals are still living, and they might even frequent the autograph show circuit or participate in "private signing" sessions arranged by dealers. In other words, the missing signatures are often still obtainable. Should they be added to the ball?

First of all, virtually no collector would frown on adding a missing signature to a team ball that was originally signed as many as five or even ten years earlier. In such cases, nearly all collectors would deem the delay in the addition of the signature to be immaterial to value or condition.

On the question of adding a signature more than ten years after the original signing of a ball, there is a difference of opinion. Some collectors are purists, and they take the view that any signature added a substantial period of time after a ball was originally signed diminishes the value of the ball. Other collectors freely add signatures to team balls 30, 40, and even 50 years after the original signing, concerned more about completeness than keeping the ball in its pure original state.

Many collectors, including the authors, take a balanced view. Rather than applying any fixed rule, borrowing from the law, the authors suggest that a balancing test be used by a collector in determining whether a signature should be added to a team ball: the advantages of adding a signature should be weighed against the disadvantages. In applying the test, the following factors should be considered:

If you choose to send a ball to a show promoter to be signed rather than having it signed in your presence, make sure that you follow the promoter's shipping instructions carefully, place specific and brief instructions on the ball holder itself, and tape the pen that you want to be used to the holder as well. Even if you do those things, be prepared for possible disappointment. Many promoters are rushed when conducting signings and are not as careful as they should be in following customers' instructions. For that reason, it is advisable never to send a particularly treasured or valuable ball away for signing; if you must add a signature, try to wait until you have an opportunity to have it done personally or have a trusted friend do it for you.

There are other methods of obtaining a signature. Some players still sign autographs before or after games or in hotel lobbies. In addition, it is sometimes possible to obtain a signature by writing to the player.[4] It is always advisable to write to a player in advance and ask whether he would be willing to sign a baseball before shipping it. If the player agrees to sign it, the collector should always include a box for the player to use in returning the ball as well as return postage. The collector should also include the pen with which the ball is to be signed, brief instructions, and a thank-you note.

Notes

1. Robert S. Pindyck and Daniel L. Rubinfeld, *Microeconomics* (5th ed.) (Upper Saddle River, N.J.: Prentice Hall, 2001), 7.
2. Ibid., 9–10.
3. Ibid., 20.
4. The best source for addresses of present and former players, managers, and coaches is R. J. Smalling, *The Baseball Autograph Collector's Handbook* (15th ed.) (Ames, Iowa: R. J. Smalling, 2009). See http://www.baseballaddresses.com/coverpage.html.

EIGHT

OBTAINING TEAM BASEBALLS

Until the rise of an organized market for sports memorabilia in the 1980s, ownership of team balls was mainly limited to players, their families, team employees, and friends and relatives of members of those groups. Certainly there were a few pioneer collectors who managed to find balls through personal contacts with players, estate sales, and the like, but that was exceptional. Most of the rest of the population, including baseball fans, did not know that team balls existed, let alone own one. There were hints along the way, and baseball fans might have seen facsimile balls at stadium concession stands beginning around 1950, but most did not realize that the real thing existed. Even if they knew that teams did actually sign baseballs, they generally had no idea of how to obtain one.

In the 1970s, a market finally developed for sports memorabilia, and card shows were inaugurated, which later expanded to become full-blown sports memorabilia shows. The number of dealers exploded, and team balls began to enter the marketplace as those who owned them realized that they had value. As baseball fans became aware that team balls existed and could be purchased, more and more people began collecting them, a trend that led to rising values and an ever-growing number of dealers and auction firms searching for more product to sell. That continuing cycle has led to the maturing market of today, in which more team balls are constantly entering the market and the collector base continues to expand.

Since the inception of the market, there has been a proliferation of sources from which team balls may be acquired. This chapter discusses those sources and offers tips for dealing with each of them.

DEALERS

Many sports memorabilia dealers buy and sell team balls. They range from individual dealers who buy and sell in their spare time to larger companies. Dealers vary greatly in their levels of knowledge of team balls, and it is recommended that a collector first establish relationships with a few well-known and respected dealers and then ask those dealers (or other experienced collectors) for references when dealing with a lesser-known dealer for the first time, especially when contemplating the purchase of an expensive item.

Some dealers advertise team balls for sale in memorabilia publications. Many of the smaller dealers do not advertise but rather sell their items at shows and through e-mail lists of customers that they develop over time. More and more dealers are also using Internet auctions and establishing their own websites in order to market their inventory.

Reputable dealers who sell team balls often accept a prompt return of a ball for a refund if the buyer is not satisfied. The exact terms of the return privilege should be stated in a bill of sale or a certificate of authenticity issued by the dealer every time a purchase is made, particularly the time period of the privilege and whether it is dependent on the item description having been incorrect or the item being "proved" to be non-authentic (see Chapter Five). The attractiveness of a team ball to a collector is a subjective matter, and therefore it is recommended that a collector never purchase a ball without either having seen sharp color images of the ball or having the right to return it. A collector should be very suspicious of any dealer who states that he or she will not accept a return. Of course, courtesy should always be practiced, and a collector should never purchase a ball with the intention of returning it. A collector should always obtain at least a detailed verbal description of the ball and make sure that it sounds satisfactory before purchasing it. With the widespread use of digital cameras and e-mail, it should almost always be possible to see digital images of a ball before concluding the purchase.

It is worthwhile for a collector to establish relationships with as many dealers as possible, and to let them know the kinds of items he or she is seeking. Very often, in order to avoid the cost and delay inherent in advertising, upon receiving a new item a dealer will contact selected customers who he or she believes might have an interest in the item.

AUCTIONS

By far the most popular method of buying and selling team balls is by auction. In fact, auction has become almost the sole means of selling rare, high-priced team balls. The consignors prefer the auction format for rare team balls because they believe that they will receive the highest price as a result of competition among bidders. Those who run the auctions like the format because it eliminates the cost of carrying inventory—generally they pay the consignor only when the ball has been sold and payment has been received from the purchaser.

Whereas traditionally auctions were live public events at which items were put on the block and sold to the highest bidder in the auction room, today several different auction formats are in use. Some elements are common to all auctions. All sports memorabilia auctions produce a catalog in advance of the sale, which describes and usually depicts the items to be auctioned. The auction date, rules, and terms and conditions are also included. The catalog might be posted on a website, printed in hard copy, or both. All auctions charge a fee to either the consignor or the buyer, or most commonly to both, for the service of performing the auction. That fee is commonly a percentage of the final selling price of the item, and the "seller's fee" is typically 10–15%. The fee charged to the buyer (generally called the "buyer's premium") is generally between 15% and 20% and has risen over the years. All auctions sell items to the highest bidder. That is where the similarities among auctions end.

Internet Auctions

The latest exciting innovation in auctions is the Internet auction, and it has rapidly become the prevailing method of auctioning sports memorabilia. Since widespread public use of the Internet began in the late 1990s, auction firms have been creating auction websites and extending their operations to the World Wide Web. Some of those sites (most notably eBay) serve as auction "conduits" for buyers and sellers of a broad range of items. They provide places where sellers can list, and provide photographs of, the items they are selling. Buyers can visit the sites, perform searches, view items, ask sellers questions by e-mail, and place bids. The auction sites automatically control the auction process under published rules using their software.

Conduit auctions have varying fee structures, but generally they charge the seller a nominal listing fee when the item is initially listed for auction, and then a small percentage of the final selling price of the item when it sells. Generally buyers are not charged a "buyer's premium" as in the case of live auctions and specialized sports memorabilia Internet auctions.

Every kind of item imaginable is now sold by Internet auction—from paintings to real estate. Sports memorabilia, including team balls, predictably make up one of the most popular categories of Internet auction items.

Although the first entrants into the Internet auction business were start-up companies, many of the traditional live and telephone sports memorabilia auction firms have recognized the tremendous potential of the Internet and have incorporated it into their businesses. Most of them now have websites with information about their companies and schedules of upcoming auctions, and many of them now offer on-line illustrated catalogs and Internet bidding while maintaining their traditional role as auction houses—taking control of the merchandise, authentication, cataloging, guaranteeing authenticity, receiving payments from buyers, arranging shipping, and distributing proceeds to sellers. They have maintained their basic fee structure of charging both seller's fees and buyer's premiums.

The Internet is clearly a revolutionary venue for the marketing of team balls. It has made the market much more efficient and reduced transaction costs for buyers and sellers. It allows the immediate listing of an item for sale without the cost and delay of printing and mailing a physical catalog. It allows for the marketing of an item to everyone who has Internet access —a virtually unlimited audience. It provides a very inexpensive means of making high-quality photographs of a ball available. It also enables more team balls to reach the market, as people who have them but are not involved in the hobby now have a convenient means of selling them. Finally, it has the potential to expand the number of collectors, as those who were unaware of the availability of team balls see them offered on the Internet and become interested in collecting.

The Internet is not a panacea, however. Some "conduit" sites have become a haven for fraud, as unscrupulous (and often anonymous) sellers use them to foist non-authentic autographed baseballs—mostly forged single-signature balls, but increasingly team balls—on the unsuspecting. In the case of team balls, the Internet suffers from the same pitfalls as the general team ball market, such as clubhouse signatures and facsimile balls. Those pitfalls are magnified, however, because the knowledgeable dealer or auction house, with a reputation to protect, is sometimes not present in the transaction and therefore cannot act as the gatekeeper to prevent nonauthentic items from reaching the market. If *caveat emptor* is the watchword for the traditional team ball market, it applies doubly to the Internet. The Internet is like the popular image of the Wild West adapted to the computer age—law and order is hard to come by, and practically anything goes. When using conduit auction sites, it is even more vital that collectors have the knowledge to authenticate team balls themselves, or, if they do not, that they seek expert assistance.

Conduit auction sites are certainly excellent sources of interesting and authentic team balls. They will never replace the traditional auction firms, however, precisely because those firms will always offer value to buyers and sellers by authenticating merchandise, maximizing marketing opportunities, and providing a reputable middleman to qualify bidders and handle payments. Many have adopted the Internet format, so that they offer the best of both worlds—the advantages of the Internet and the traditional auction firm combined. They might feel some pressure to reduce their fee structure somewhat to remain competitive, but their services should always command a premium over the Internet conduit auctions because they offer more value for the money.

Live Auctions

The traditional live auction is still alive and well, but with the advent of Internet auctions the number of live auctions for sports memorabilia has declined. Sports memorabilia (including team balls) are still sold by a number of different large and small auction firms at live auction on a regular basis. Those firms often provide a solid guarantee of authenticity, which makes them especially attractive to beginning collectors. The rules of a live auction are usually fairly simple: the bidder has the choice of bidding by (1) attending the auction and bidding in person, (2) participating in real time by prearranged telephone bidding (a representative of the auction house calls the bidder when the item comes up at the live auction and bids

or on websites offering to purchase signed baseballs. Most newspapers have a "Collectibles" or "Antiques and Collectibles" classification that is well suited for such ads. Do not expect someone to call with a box of Yankees team balls from the 1920s, but if you run such ads consistently you might very well pick up some interesting items for your collection.

If you are looking only for vintage items, it is highly recommended that you mention a time period in your classified ads, such as "Pre-1980 Only." Otherwise, you will likely be flooded with calls about newer items in which you have no interest.

ANTIQUE SHOWS, FLEA MARKETS, AND ESTATE SALES

Team balls are not commonly found at antique shows, flea markets, or estate sales, but they do turn up at such events occasionally. It is not advisable to attend such an event solely to look for team balls, especially if attendance involves a significant travel distance, because the chances of finding them are very slim. If a team ball collector is present at such an event, however, he or she should certainly keep an eye out for baseballs. Once in a while a real find is made—and those finds can be very exciting.

CONCLUSION

Assembling an impressive team ball collection requires a significant amount of time and effort. The best way to do it as quickly and cost-effectively as possible is to seek out all of the diverse sources from which balls can be obtained (within the bounds of prudence). Tracking down rare and interesting pieces is part of the fun of collecting.

Considering all of the time and resources required to build a prized collection, the preservation, storage, and management of a collection are of great importance. Those are the subjects of our final chapter.

NINE

PRESERVATION, STORAGE, AND COLLECTION MANAGEMENT

Team balls are very fragile objects. They are not fragile in the sense that they are breakable; obviously the ball was designed to withstand being hit hard by a bat repeatedly. Rather, they are fragile in the sense that the features that make them attractive to a collector—first and foremost the signatures, but also the original white, fresh appearance of the leather—are vulnerable to many perils. Exposure to light can fade signatures, handling can cause wear and discoloration, exposure to liquid or high humidity can make the ink bleed, heat and exposure to air can cause toning of the surface, and insects and rodents can eat away at the leather and the stitching.

The very interaction between the ink and the surface of the ball can cause degradation, and such interaction is sometimes uncontrollable and unpredictable. If a dozen identical baseballs are purchased, signed by a team with the same pen, stored in ideal conditions for ten years, and then examined, it is possible that at least a few of the balls will have suffered some degradation (perhaps toning or ink bleeding), while others might remain in mint condition. Baseballs are designed for use in games, not for signing, and they are satisfactory but not optimal media for autographs.

Fortunately, when properly handled and stored, most team balls do not degrade significantly over time. Certain techniques of storage and care should be used to maximize the chances of effective preservation, and those techniques are the subject of this chapter. It is important for a collector to learn those techniques and to practice them scrupulously. The failure to do so can have disastrous consequences for the appearance and value of a collection. The related topic of collection management will also be covered.

PRESERVATION AND STORAGE

Handling

One cardinal rule of team ball preservation is that handling should be avoided as much as possible. Everyone has dirt and oil on his or her hands, and handling a team ball can transfer that dirt and oil to the surface of the ball and cause discoloration of the surface or smudging of the signatures. Handling can also cause wear to the signatures by literally rubbing off some of the ink. If a ball must be handled, it should be handled as briefly as possible after washing and thoroughly drying one's hands; it should be held only by the stitching, with one's fingertips; and the signed surfaces should never be touched. Use of clean white cotton gloves also should be considered. Optimally, a team ball should be handled only when it is being placed in a proper storage container, and seldom, if ever, again.

One sometimes sees pictures of team balls for sale in Internet auctions with the seller's hand wrapped around it, presumably to hold it in a certain position for photographing, when simply resting the ball on a clean, nonporous surface would have sufficed. It is enough to make a collector cringe.

Storage

Team balls should be stored in clean holders made of a clear, nonporous material such as acrylic. A number of such holders on the market are designed specifically for baseballs. The oldest style of baseball holder is the spherical clear plastic holder set into a round plastic base, which is usually a metallic gold color. The most popular holder today is the ball cube, of which there are three basic designs: (1) a clear plastic cube consisting of two interlocking U-shaped pieces (by far the most popular design); (2) a five-sided cube with a snap-on clear cap forming the sixth side (through which the ball is inserted); and (3) two interlocking open-ended five-sided cubes. The reason for the popularity of the cube is that it is very stable and affords a view of the entire surface of the ball without having to manipulate the position of the ball inside the holder. Another holder that has gained popularity with some collectors is a cylindrical holder with a removable clear cap. Those ball holders are inexpensive; they can usually be purchased for approximately $1.50–$2.00 per holder. All of them perform the function of protecting the ball while still permitting it to be viewed. The authors suggest purchasing a case or two of holders and keeping them on hand for use as needed.

A collector should be particularly careful when placing a ball in a ball cube of the interlocking U-shaped design. When sliding the two pieces together, care must be taken to prevent the edges of the pieces from scuffing the ball. The best way to avoid that kind of damage is to place the ball in one half of the cube, set it on a table, and then carefully slide the other half of the cube into place while slightly bending the two moving edges away from the ball's surfaces with one's fingertips. A collector also should be careful when using holders that employ snap-on caps (whether cubical or cylindrical), because sometimes the cap can become dislodged and fall off if the ball rolls up against it.

Several manufacturers offer holders or cabinets that can house multiple baseballs for display. Some of the larger units are designed to be hung on a wall like a picture frame, and they have shelves inside with rows of small pedestals on which the balls are placed, which are often made of plastic or wood. Such multiple-ball display units typically have a clear acrylic door on the front. The advantage of those units is that they can be very attractive and functional means of displaying a collection. A disadvantage is that the balls are not held in place (they remain on the pedestals solely by the force of gravity), and if the unit falls or even tilts the balls within could easily fall off the pedestals and be damaged. Another disadvantage is that the use of such a display unit might subject the balls to long-term exposure to damaging light (see the next section).

A team ball should never be stored for any length of time in a box or other container in which it will be in direct contact with a porous surface such as cardboard or tissue paper, especially when the ball has been signed within the preceding five years. Direct and sustained contact with a porous surface before the ink has completely dried and set (which can take years) can cause the ink to bleed on the surface of the ball.

Protection from Light

Light is the greatest enemy of signed baseballs. Exposure to light over a length of time, particularly the ultraviolet component of sunlight and fluorescent light, can cause the signatures to fade severely. The technical reason is that ultraviolet light causes photodegradation of the ink. Ink contains dyes and pigments that give it color; ultraviolet light causes the color molecules in those dyes and pigments to break into weakly colored fragments, thus producing the appearance of fading. Heat accelerates those reactions and thus the fading process. In contrast to sunlight and fluorescent light, incandescent light contains little or no ultraviolet radiation, and in moderation it should not cause appreciable fading of signatures on a baseball.

Prolonged exposure to light can also cause the surface of a baseball to turn tan or brown over time; that process is referred to as "toning," and baseballs that have turned tan or brown are referred to as "toned" (or, more specifically, "lightly," "moderately," or "heavily" toned). Toning can also be caused by exposure to tobacco smoke, or simply by the natural aging process of the leather cover of the baseball, but light also can have an impact. Sometimes toning is unavoidable because it results from materials and substances used in manufacturing the baseball.

It is never advisable to leave a team ball out for display unless measures are taken to shade or filter out any ultraviolet light. Acrylic naturally affords some limited filtration, and thus it is advisable for collectors to seek out and use ball holders that are made of acrylic. Some manufacturers produce ball holders that are claimed to have ultraviolet filtering properties, but before relying on the effectiveness of such filtering, a collector should request the results of independent testing of the filtering effectiveness of those holders over the long term. The authors are not willing to risk a prized team ball just to find out if the manufacturer's claims are valid, although if such a holder were shown by scientific testing to afford significant protection from ultraviolet light, it would certainly be advisable to use it for valuable baseballs, even at a cost several times that of a regular holder without such protection.

The most effective way to prevent fading from exposure to light is obviously to store the ball so that no light reaches it. The easiest way to accomplish that is to store the ball cube or other holder, with the ball inside, in the cardboard box in which it was originally sold or in a dark cabinet, safe, or bank safe-deposit box. A collector might also consider purchasing large, archival boxes made of acid-free and lignin-free materials for storage of balls in acrylic holders. Such an approach is not very satisfying for a collector who wants to display his or her collection, but it is the safest method of preservation.

The authors have heard stories of (and even witnessed) fanatical collectors shutting off all of their lights and pulling out their collection for viewing in nearly total darkness. It is not necessary to go to those extreme lengths, but in displaying team balls every collector should have a healthy respect for light and the damage it can cause. The best advice is to store a team ball in an acrylic holder and keep it away from sunlight and all other sources of fluorescent light. Collectors should also watch the market for the introduction of ball holders that have a credible, scientifically valid claim to providing filtration of ultraviolet light.

Protection from Extremes of Temperature, Humidity, and Moisture

Temperature and humidity are also significant threats to team balls. As noted earlier, heat speeds up the fading process caused by exposure to ultraviolet light. Exposure to excessive heat or humidity can also accelerate the toning of the baseball's surface. Exposure to high humidity can cause ink signatures on a baseball to bleed over time. Exposure to freezing temperatures can also degrade a team ball.

Team balls should be stored in places where temperature and humidity are controlled at all times. They should never be stored in an attic or storage facility without a controlled climate, or in any location where they might come into contact with water or excessive humidity, such as in an underground basement. Never allow a team ball to become wet.

To Coat or Not to Coat

The practice of applying a protective coating of shellac or other clear sealant with the goal of preserving the signatures on a team ball began at the dawn of signed baseballs in the early part of the twentieth century, reached its peak in the 1930s and 1940s, and then began to diminish to the point where it was relatively uncommon by the 1960s. The coating of baseballs has continued to be practiced, however, right down to the present day. Several different substances have been used through the years, including shellac, acrylic, and, believe it or not, nail polish and hair spray.

Some collectors frown on coated team balls, considering the coating to be a condition flaw per se and thus a detriment to value. The authors take a balanced view, as do the vast majority of collectors: each coated ball should be evaluated on its own merits. Some coatings are better than others, and those that are thin, even, and not cracked, chipped, or discolored can very effectively preserve the signatures and the ball over time when otherwise they might have degraded. A good coating can actually enhance the appearance of a team ball by making the signatures appear darker and more vivid. The authors have seen many older team balls that were coated soon after signing, and, as a result, look as they did on the day they were signed. Figure 9.1 shows an example of such a ball, a 1963 San Francisco Giants team ball that has been preserved in its original state by a good coating.

An important question is whether a collector should ever apply a coating to a team ball that is not already coated when he or she obtains it. On that subject, a conservative approach makes the most sense. The decision should be approached very much like one regarding elective surgery. Too many things can go wrong when coating a baseball; for example, the ball's round surface can cause the coating to run, and the chemical interaction

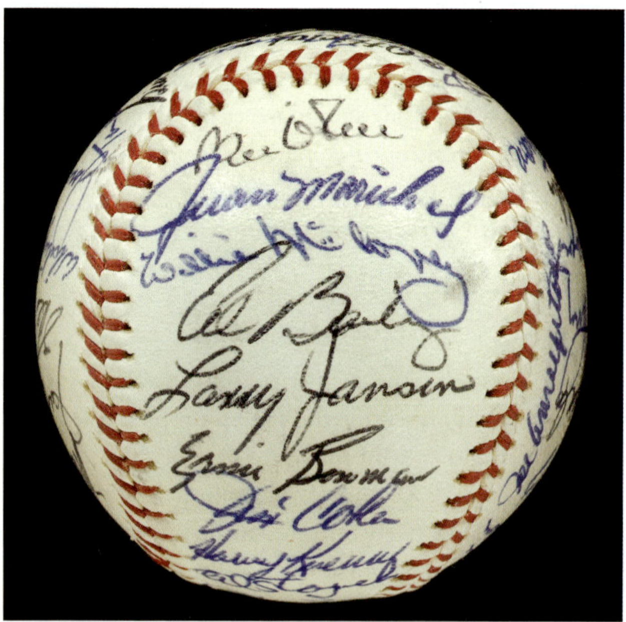

Figure 9.1. 1963 San Francisco Giants team ball with perfectly preserved signatures owing to a clear coating applied shortly after the ball was signed.

between the solvent in which the coating is dissolved and the ink of the signatures is unpredictable—it might cause the signatures to bleed or even fade before it evaporates. Therefore, an old adage applies to coating a team ball: "if it ain't broke, don't fix it."

Sometimes, however, natural processes cause the signatures on a team ball to fade or change color. For example, for some reason (possibly oxidization) black ballpoint ink signatures on a baseball have a tendency to turn brown or even brownish-red within a few years after signing. A collector should examine his or her collection periodically to see if any particular ball is suffering such deterioration. If so, the collector should continue to monitor the ball and should seriously consider whether it might be worth the risk of applying a coating.

If a coating appears to be necessary, a clear, colorless acrylic spray coating is recommended, such as Krylon Crystal Clear, which should be applied in no more than two or three very quick, light, even coats on each half of the ball, allowing each coat to dry thoroughly before turning the ball to coat the other half. The coating should be applied in very short bursts of no more than a few seconds each, rapidly moving the can from side to side or in a circular motion approximately 10–12 inches from the ball in order to apply a light, even coating. Do not brush a coating onto a ball, because the mechanical action of brushing might smear the signatures; always use a spray coating. Acrylic is recommended because it will not darken (or "yellow") over time.

The coating should never be allowed to accumulate (or become "puddled") on the surface of the ball; as noted earlier, puddling can cause bleeding of the ink before the solvent evaporates, and it might also discolor the ball's surface. Over-spraying might also cause the coating to drip down the spherical surface of the ball. It is advisable to practice applying a spray coating to a cheap unsigned baseball (or one on which some test writing has been applied) before spraying an actual signed baseball.

We do not know the long-term effects of applying a coating such as Krylon Crystal Clear to a baseball, but in tests conducted by one of the authors, signatures on baseballs coated 12 years before the publication of this book have been well preserved with no yellowing or other undesirable effects. There is certainly some risk involved, however, and the decision of whether to apply the coating should be made only after careful consideration, and perhaps only after consulting an expert.

COLLECTION MANAGEMENT

There are many good reasons for keeping detailed records of a collection. For instance, if the collection has significant monetary value, the collector might want to obtain insurance coverage, and insurance companies that insure collectibles often require a detailed list of the items to be covered by the policy. In addition, if a ball is ever sold, for tax purposes it is important to have detailed information on the original date of purchase and the purchase price. If there is a theme to the collection, it is also very useful to have a handy list of the items that have already been obtained so that the items still needed may be readily ascertained. Keeping detailed information on a collection also facilitates keeping track of its value and whereabouts.

For smaller collections (i.e., fewer than 50 balls), a handwritten list or computer spreadsheet should be sufficient. For each ball, the following information should be recorded:

- Year and team
- Date acquired
- Price paid
- Identity of the seller
- Number of signatures
- Type of baseball
- Storage location
- List of signatures

If the ball has a certificate or letter of authenticity or provenance, that should also be recorded. Any other items of special significance, such as a championship won by the team or the presence of a rookie signature of a famous player, should also be noted.

For larger collections, it is recommended that a collector consider acquiring one of the computer software programs designed to help collectors keep track of their collections. Those programs are inexpensive and readily available, and they often have useful features such as a search function and the ability to insert digital photographs into an item listing. As with any important electronic data, the data created with those programs should be backed up frequently, and a hard copy of the collection list should be printed periodically and stored in a safe place.

For all collections (and particularly large ones), it is advisable to assign a serial or inventory number to each ball and to include the number in the collection listing. A label showing the number should then be placed on the ball holder, or on the box in which the ball and holder are kept. The authors prefer to use sequential serial numbers that begin with a letter that designates the category in which the ball fits (e.g., A for All-Star team balls or W for World Championship team balls), but any numbering system that enables the collector to match a ball with the data on his or her collection list will suffice.

One piece of additional advice: begin keeping detailed records of your purchases as soon as you start collecting, and be scrupulous about recording new purchases as they are made. If a collector procrastinates, he or she will eventually find the information either gone or hopelessly scattered, and it will be very difficult, if not impossible, to reconstruct proper records.

GALLERY

A SELECTION OF HISTORICALLY SIGNIFICANT TEAM BASEBALLS

1920 Brooklyn Robins team ball (National League Champions). This ball was likely signed at the 1920 World Series, and includes the signatures of Charles Ebbets (the Robins' owner) and August Herrmann (president of the National Baseball Commission, the predecessor position to commissioner of baseball).

1920 Cleveland Indians team ball (World Champions). Signed at the 1920 World Series, a best-of-nine contest in which baseball began its recovery from the 1919 World Series gambling scandal.

1925 Washington Senators team ball (American League Champions). The defending World Champions who signed this ball succumbed to the Pittsburgh Pirates, marking the first time that a team had come back from a 3-1 deficit to prevail in a best-of-seven World Series.

1926 New York Yankees team ball (American League Champions). After succumbing to the St. Louis Cardinals in the 1926 World Series, eight victorious Series appearances would pass for the Yankees before they found themselves on the losing side again—in 1942.

1926 St. Louis Cardinals team ball (World Champions). This team featured an amazing six future Hall of Famers.

1930 St. Louis Cardinals team ball (National League Champions), surely one of the best-preserved team balls of the era.

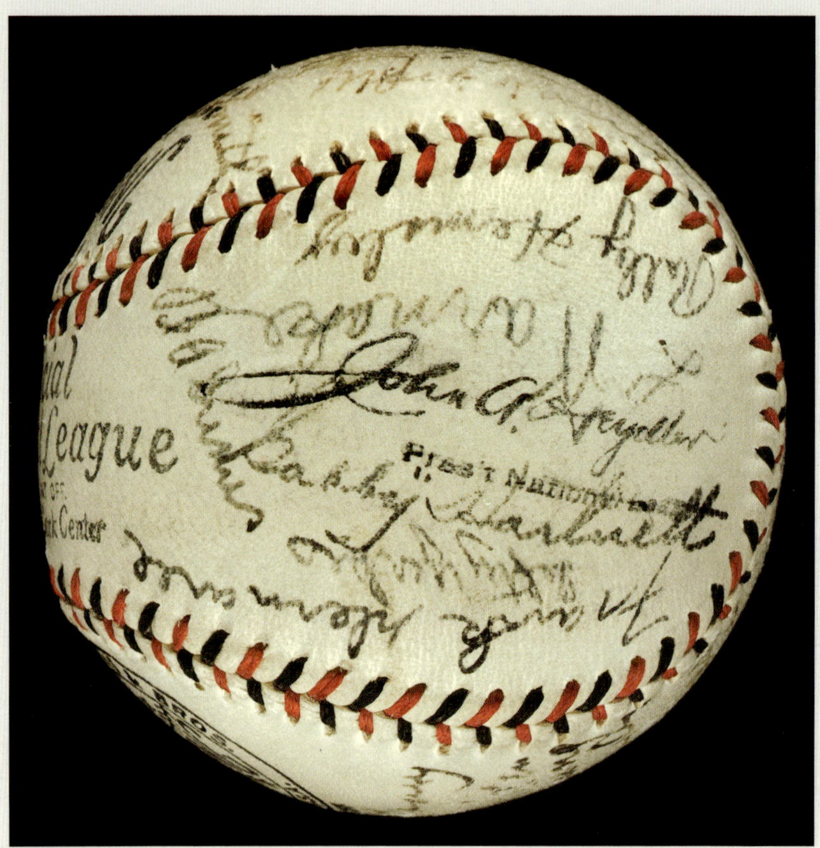

1932 Chicago Cubs team ball (National League Champions), the team against which Babe Ruth allegedly called his shot in the 1932 World Series.

1932 New York Yankees team ball (World Champions), dating from the height of Babe Ruth's career—and the size of his signature.

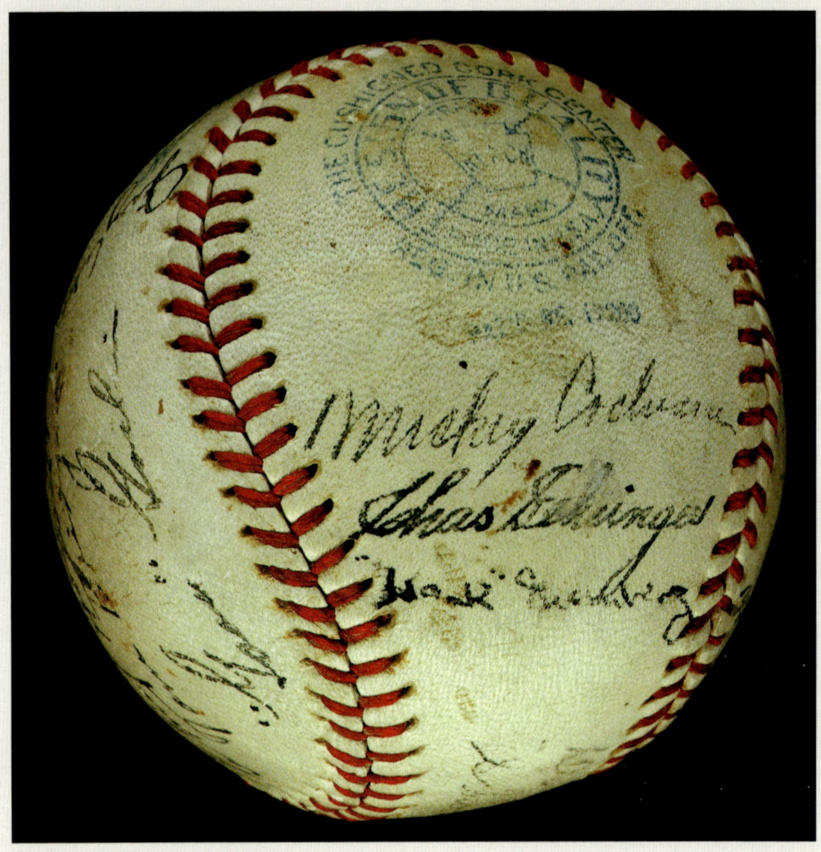

1935 Detroit Tigers team ball (World Champions), signed by the Tigers' first World Championship team.

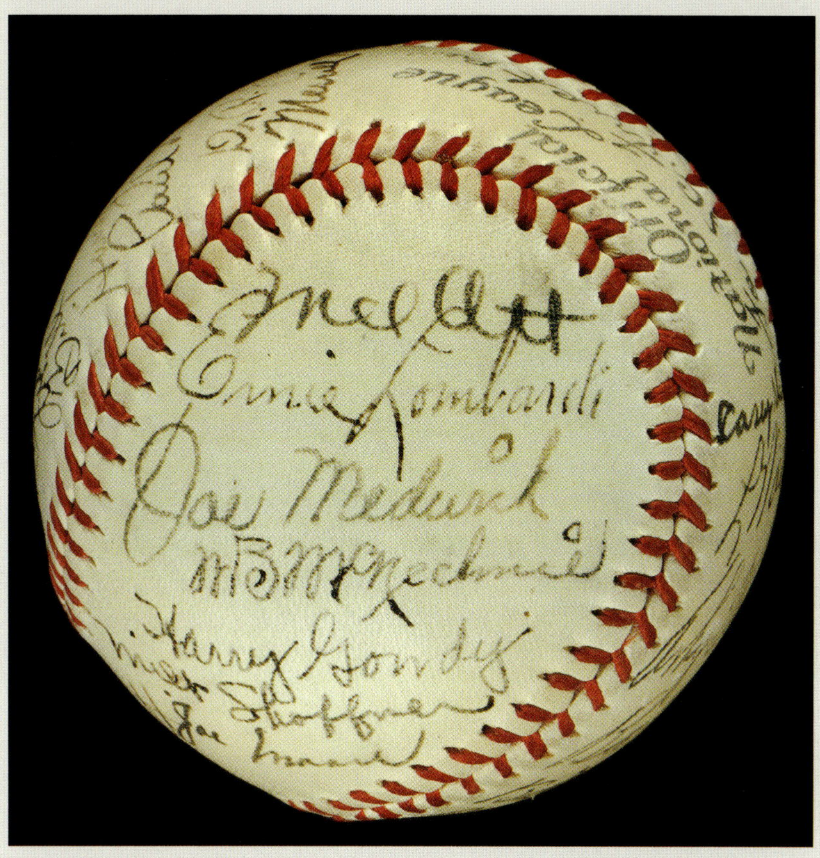

1940 National League All-Star team ball. This team orchestrated the first shutout in All-Star Game history, prevailing 4-0 over the American League squad.

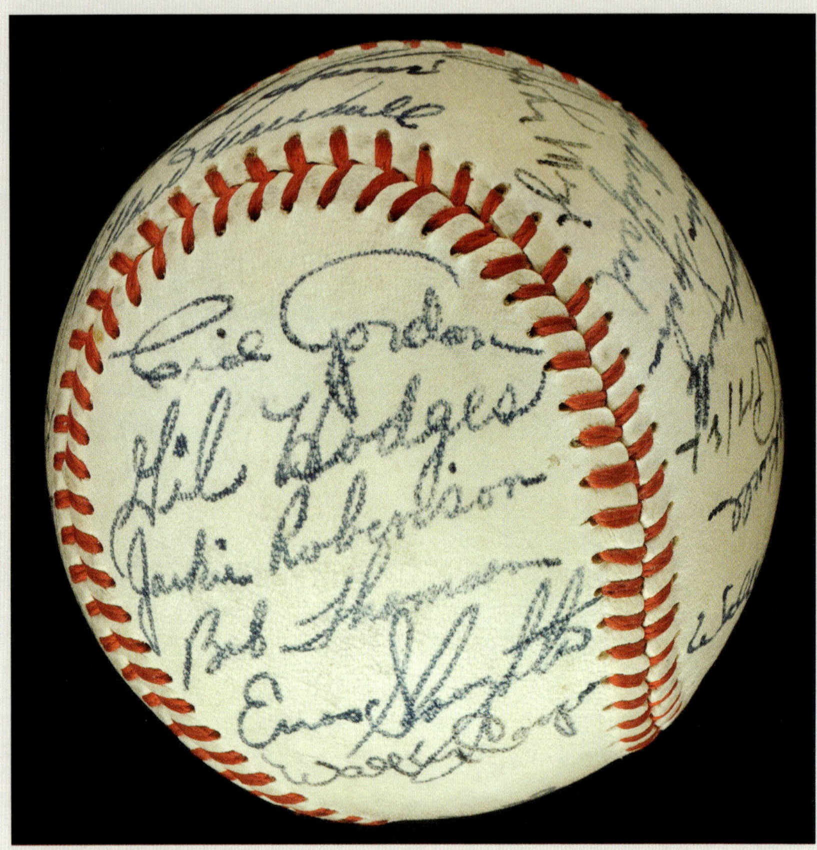

1949 National League All-Star team ball. This was the first All-Star Game that included African-American players.

1950 Philadelphia Phillies team ball (National League Champions), called the "Whiz Kids" because of their average age of 26.

1951 New York Giants team ball (National League Champions), from Willie Mays' Rookie of the Year season.

1951 New York Yankees team ball (World Champions), from the only season in which Joe DiMaggio and Mickey Mantle were teammates.

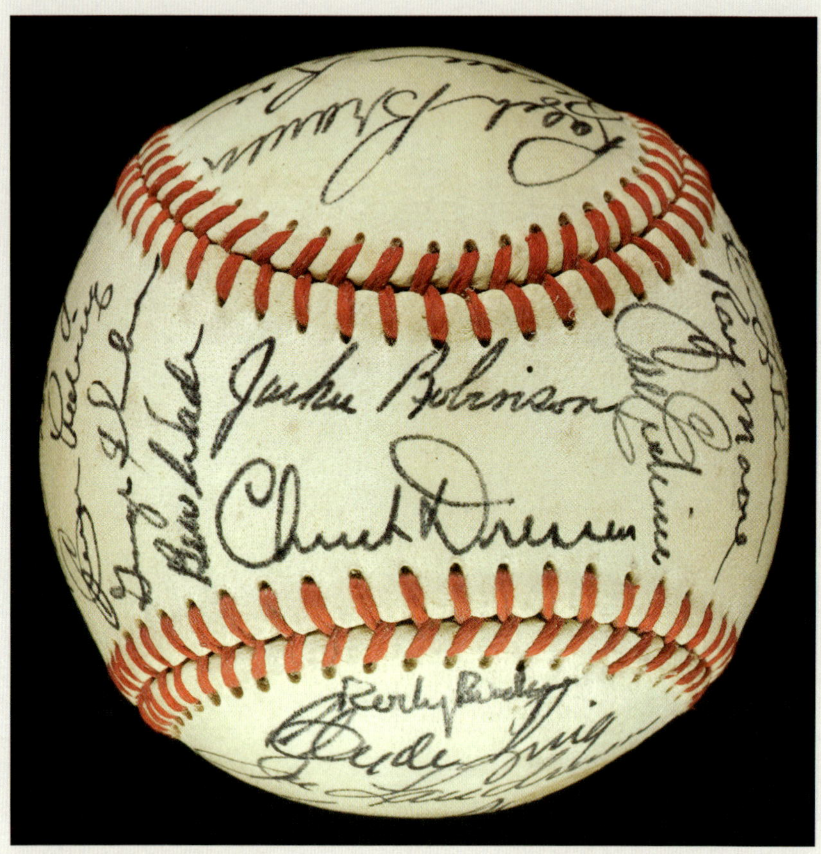

1952 Brooklyn Dodgers team ball (National League Champions). Note the rare sweet spot signature of Jackie Robinson.

1956 Brooklyn Dodgers team ball (National League Champions), from the final year of Jackie Robinson's Hall of Fame career. This team included an astounding eight Hall of Famers (including coach Billy Herman), six of whose signatures are visible above.

1957 Milwaukee Braves team ball (World Champions), with an amazing 38 original signatures, including 1957 National League Most Valuable Player Hank Aaron and Cy Young Award winner Warren Spahn.

1958 New York Yankees team ball (World Champions). Note the just-signed appearance of the blue ballpoint signatures after over 50 years, a testament to the preservation that is possible when proper storage techniques are employed.

1959 Chicago White Sox team ball (American League Champions). Note the signature of owner Bill Veeck—very rare on a team ball—on the left side.

1961 New York Yankees team ball (World Champions), featuring the signatures of Mickey Mantle and Roger Maris, who battled for the single-season home run title in 1961. Maris set a mark of 61 that lasted for 37 years and won the American League Most Valuable Player award.

1962 New York Yankees team ball (World Champions). The Yankees defeated the San Francisco Giants in a very competitive seven-game World Series.

1967 St. Louis Cardinals team ball (World Champions), the Cardinals' second World Championship team of the decade led by Most Valuable Player Orlando Cepeda.

1970 Baltimore Orioles team ball (World Champions). The powerhouse Orioles, defending American League Champions, prevailed in the 1970 World Series against the Cincinnati Reds, who were just beginning a dynasty of their own.

1971 Pittsburgh Pirates team ball (World Champions). Note the signature of Roberto Clemente at the top of the panel just below the "Official National League" stamp.

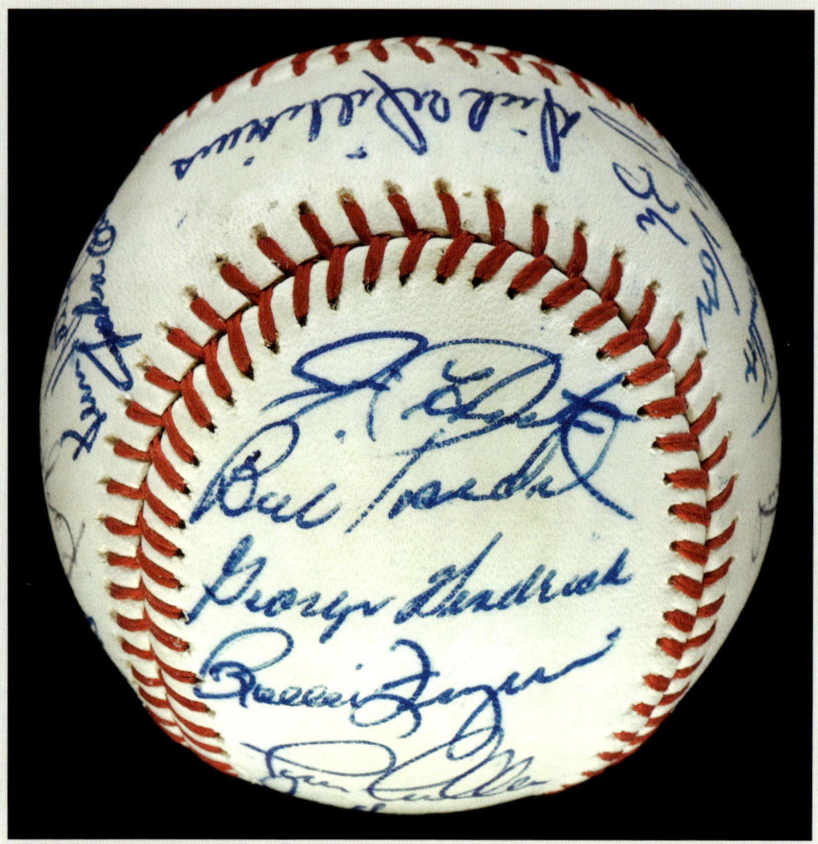

1972 Oakland Athletics team ball (World Champions). This team began a dynasty of three consecutive World Championships with a seven-game World Series win over the "Big Red Machine" in which all games but one were decided by one run.

1974 National League All-Star team ball. Note the signature of Hank Aaron along the stitching, from the season in which he broke Babe Ruth's career home run record. The Senior Circuit won this one handily, 7-2.

1975 Boston Red Sox team ball (American League Champions). Note the signature of Tony Conigliaro, whose career was tragically cut short after he was hit in the left eye by a pitch in 1967, in his final brief stint with the Red Sox.

1975 Cincinnati Reds team ball (World Champions). The "Big Red Machine" won 108 games in the regular season before besting the Boston Red Sox in an exciting seven-game World Series.

1976 New York Yankees team ball (American League Champions). This team returned the Yankees to the World Series after an 11-season drought, led by Most Valuable Player Thurman Munson.

1978 New York Yankees team ball (World Champions), repeating World Champions led by Cy Young Award winner Ron Guidry, who won 25 games against only 3 losses.

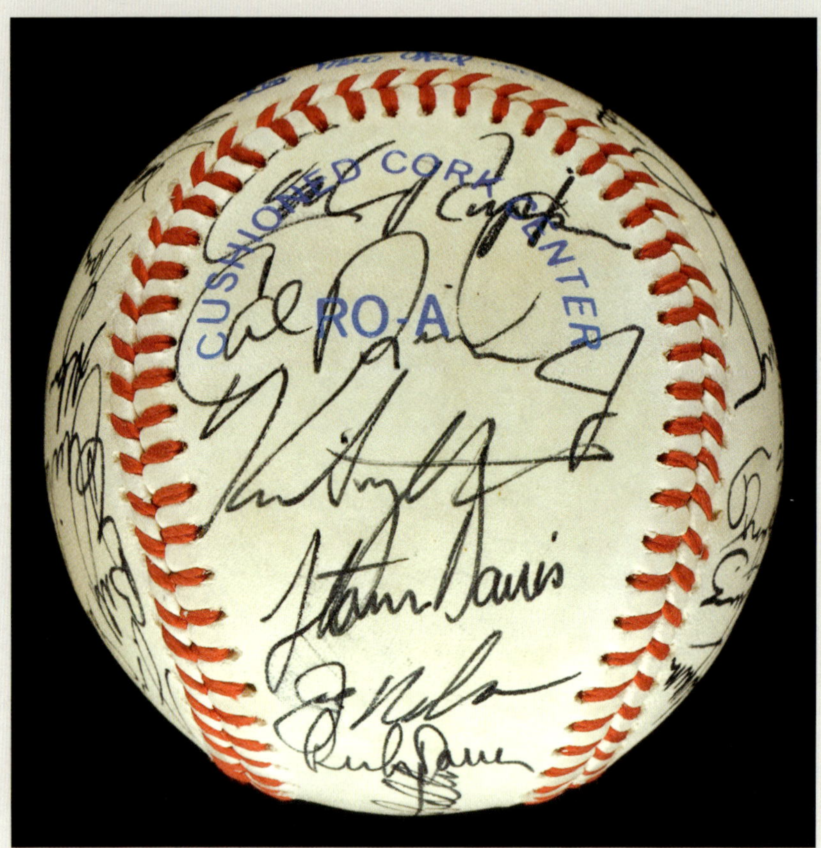

1983 Baltimore Orioles team ball (World Champions). Note the signatures of Most Valuable Player Cal Ripken, Jr., and his father (an Orioles coach) together at the top of the panel shown.

1985 Kansas City Royals team ball (World Champions), winners of the Royals' first World Championship.

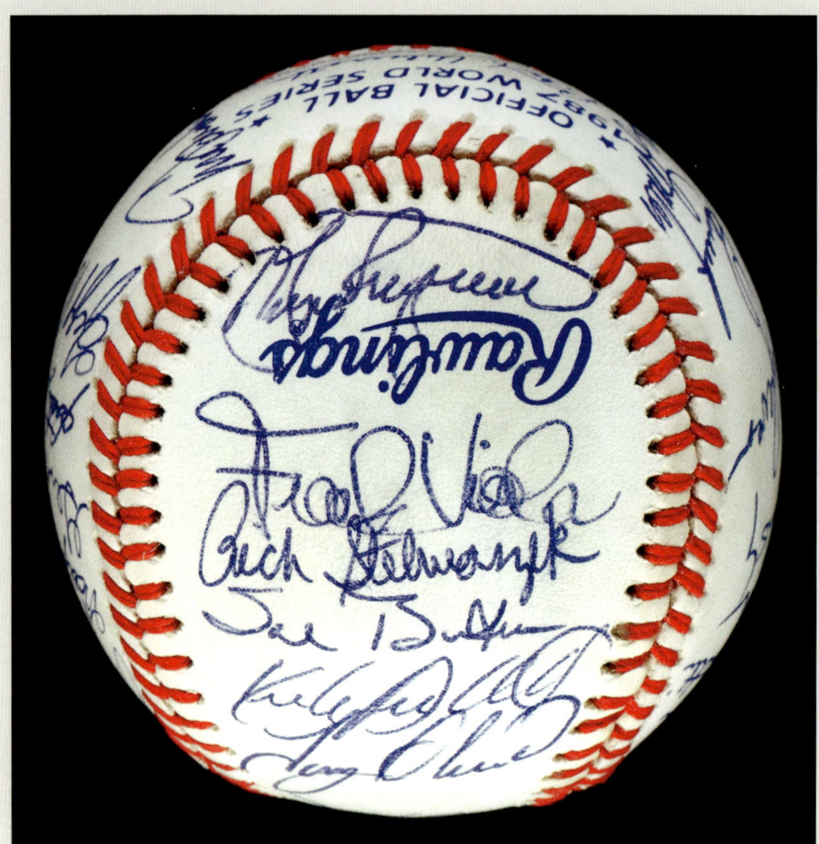

1987 Minnesota Twins team ball (World Champions), winners of the franchise's first World Championship since moving from Washington, D.C., in 1961 and changing its name from the Senators to the Twins.

1995 Atlanta Braves team ball (World Champions), the Braves' first World Championship team since moving to Atlanta in 1966.

1998 New York Yankees team ball (World Champions), winners of a record 125 games in a single season. This ball also features a possible record 41 signatures.

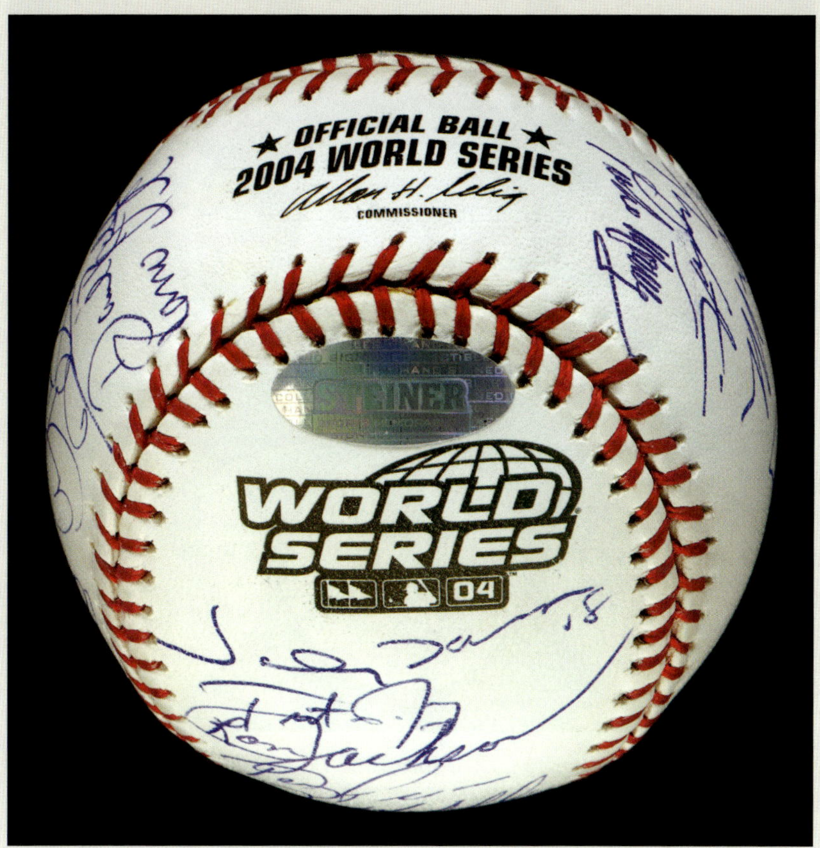

2004 Boston Red Sox team ball (World Champions), winners of the franchise's first World Championship in 86 years.

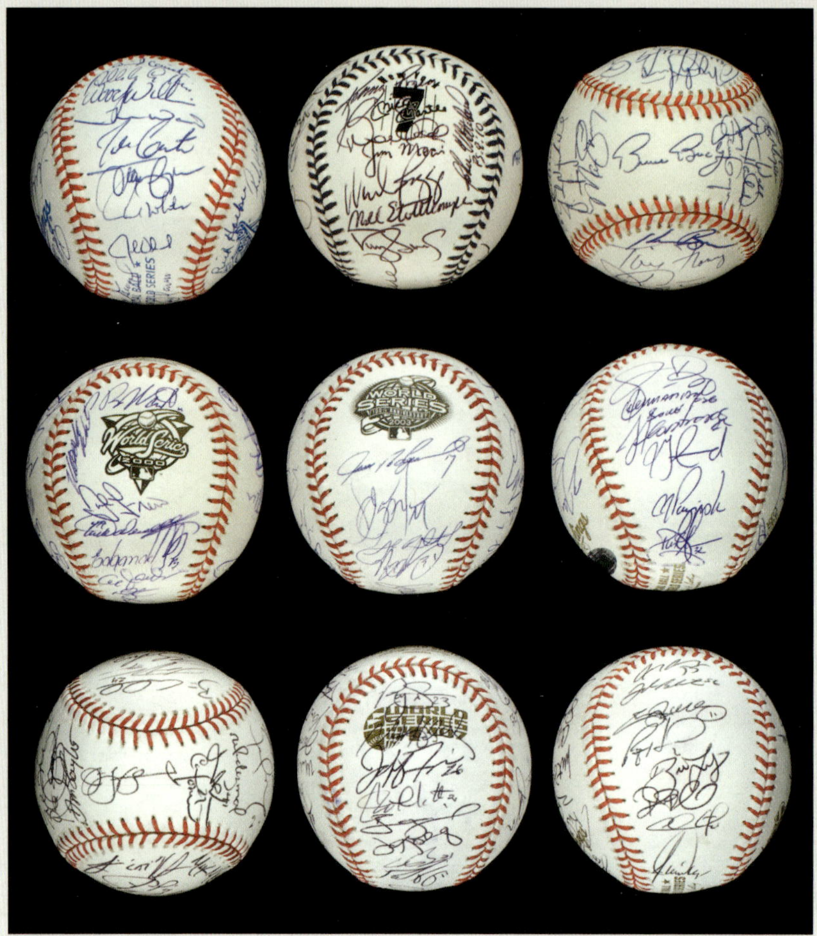

First row (left to right): 1993 Toronto Blue Jays (World Champions); 1996 New York Yankees (World Champions); 1998 San Diego Padres (National League Champions).

Second row (left to right): 2000 New York Mets (National League Champions); 2003 Florida Marlins (World Champions); 2005 Chicago White Sox (World Champions).

Third row (left to right): 2006 Detroit Tigers (American League Champions); 2007 Colorado Rockies (National League Champions); 2008 Philadelphia Phillies (World Champions).

INDEX